Table of Contents

Introduction

The influence of the Bible is impossible to ignore. Even with some of the impressive sales records of books in the last few years, the Bible remains the best-selling book of all time. Although it is an ancient text, it is an amazingly relevant source of wisdom and truth for today. While fad diets, books, and apps come and go, the enduring truths of the Bible have changed millions of lives—and they can change yours too.

In creating *100 Ways the Bible Can Change Your Life*, we haven't tried to overanalyze the Bible or rewrite its meaning for a contemporary audience. Instead, we've treated the Bible the same way countless people have treated it for thousands of years: we simply have taken it at its word. Throughout history, people have believed it, organized their lives around it, and improved their lives as a result.

These same words from this sacred book still whisper to our souls, drawing us toward something bigger than ourselves. The Bible offers powerful pearls of wisdom about daily life, our relationship to our culture, our relationship to God, and our relationship with others.

Whether you read the book all in one sitting or take one page a day and reflect on its meaning, *100 Ways the Bible Can Change Your Life* will lead you in discovering the eternal truth and wisdom of God revealed in the pages of the Bible. Join us in uncovering these timeless treasures of what you need in order to live wisely in today's world.

Christopher D. Hudson
Editor

1 Read Your Bible

The Bible is as outdated as God is. If we believe God is an ancient superstition—the creation of primitive, unenlightened people—we can write off the Bible as a collection of myths and religious nonsense.

If, on the other hand, we believe God is a living being—and one to be reckoned with—we cannot dismiss the Bible as a relic from another time. The apostle Paul explained why: "Everything in the Scriptures is God's Word. All of it is useful for teaching and helping people and for correcting them and showing them how to live" (2 Timothy 3:16).

The Bible is God's instruction to us. It contains everything he wants us to know about him, his work, and his plans for us. It is as active and viable today as he is. If we claim to follow him, we need to know his Word. But getting to know it takes time and effort. For best results, remember these four Ps.

Words of
WISDOM

2 TIMOTHY 1:13

Now follow the example of the correct teaching I gave you, and let the faith and love of Christ Jesus be your model.

Priority

Studying God's Word is the key to growing as a Christian. As followers of Christ, we're all connected. We rely on one another. We work together as one unit to follow God's instruction. The Bible calls this unit of Christians the "body" of Christ. If one of us doesn't grow, we handicap the entire body.

Purpose

We can't simply open the Bible to a random page and expect to understand its meaning. A better strategy is to approach Scripture with a specific aim in mind. For example, we may choose to read the book of Genesis to get a sense of how things got started. Or we may choose to read Matthew, Mark, Luke, and John to familiarize ourselves with Jesus' life.

Prayer

Before we open the Bible, we should ask God for three things:

- a clear head, so we can block out distractions;
- an open heart, so we can be receptive to his words;
- insight, so we can understand truths far beyond the limits of our IQs.

Permanence

With so many things constantly vying for our attention, there's a good chance that whatever we learn from the Bible today will be a distant memory by the time tomorrow rolls around. That's why it's vital to keep a written record—a journal—of our Bible investigations. ■

2 Give the Gift of Patience

What is love?

That's the question the apostle Paul tackled in 1 Corinthians 13. Near the top of the list, you'll find this:

"Love is patient" (1 Corinthians 13:4).

Being patient shows a willingness to

- cut people slack, even when they may not deserve it;
- withhold judgment when people mess up;
- give people time to grow.

Patience allows us to look past people's rough exteriors to see what's inside. Patience allows us to accept people as they are—and to resist the urge to change them.

To give someone the gift of your patience is to lay the groundwork for a deeper relationship with that person. If you have trouble giving the gift of patience to others, remind yourself that your loved ones—the people who are closest to you—give you the gift of their patience every day. ■

Love is patient and kind, neve

3 Leave No Room for Despair

"Love is always . . .
hopeful."
(1 Corinthians 13:7)

A loving approach to life leaves no room for despair. It brings a positive attitude to every situation, no matter how dire. It's a question of outlook. We choose whether we will suffer or thrive in the wake of an event.

That's not to say we should fake happiness or positivity. First, we must address and work through our natural reactions. In some cases, that may require professional help.

Beyond that, we have the choice between remaining in our grief or unhappiness and moving on—finding something else to look forward to, celebrate, or experience. ■

jealous, boastful, proud, or rude.

Work at Friendship

4

Why do you suppose Jesus emphasized forgiveness? Because he wanted us to be "nice"? Because he didn't care about justice? Because he was naïve about human evil and what we do to one another? Because "gentle Jesus, meek and mild" simply didn't grasp the horror of injustice? . . .

Forgiveness was the focal point in Christ's teaching because he knew that without genuine, profound and "to the bone" forgiveness, there is no freedom, no real joy, no peace and no release from the pain and the "root of bitterness" that destroys nations, families and individuals. He understood that the key to everything important in life is forgiveness.

Steve Brown
(adapted from KeyLife.org)

"Be kind and merciful, and forgive others, just as God forgave you because of Christ" (Ephesians 4:32).

Lasting friendship only happens with hard work. Because we are human, we are not perfect people, and that affects every area of life—including our friendships. Over time, any friendship will fall victim to disagreements, jealousy, misunderstandings, and inconsideration. And while we (or our friends) may give in to these shortcomings, that doesn't mean that the friendship is failed and worthy of being terminated.

Have you known someone who builds fast friendships but then moves on to another friend at the first sign of conflict or disagreement? Don't be that person. Friendships can deepen through adversity, grow through pain, and flourish with forgiveness. Rather than abandon someone who has hurt you, see if you can work through the issue. Sometimes lifelong friendships are born through tears of forgiveness. ■

WOULD YOU THROW AWAY A
DIAMOND BECAUSE IT PRICKED
YOU? ONE GOOD FRIEND IS
NOT TO BE WEIGHED AGAINST
ALL THE JEWELS OF ALL THE
EARTH. IF THERE IS COOLNESS
OR UNKINDNESS BETWEEN US,
LET US COME FACE TO FACE AND
HAVE IT OUT. QUICK, BEFORE
THE LOVE GROWS COLD. LIFE
IS TOO SHORT TO QUARREL IN,
OR CARRY DARK THOUGHTS OF
FRIENDS. IT IS EASY TO LOSE A
FRIEND, BUT A NEW ONE WILL
NOT COME FOR CALLING, NOR
MAKE UP FOR THE OLD ONE
WHEN HE COMES.

Leaves of Gold

DO YOUR WORK WILLINGLY, AS THOUGH YOU WERE SERVING THE LORD HIMSELF, AND NOT JUST YOUR EARTHLY MASTER. Colossians 3:23

Don't Give Worry a Foothold

5

People find stress relief in many different forms: exercise, meditation, massages.

To those we add Jesus' words in Matthew 6:25–30:

> I tell you not to worry about your life. Don't worry about having something to eat, drink, or wear. Isn't life more than food or clothing? Look at the birds in the sky! They don't plant or harvest. They don't even store grain in barns. Yet your Father in heaven takes care of them. Aren't you worth more than birds?
>
> Can worry make you live longer? Why worry about clothes? Look how the wild flowers grow. They don't work hard to make their clothes. But I tell you that Solomon with all his wealth wasn't as well clothed as one of them. God gives such beauty to everything that grows in the fields, even though it is here today and thrown into a fire tomorrow. God will surely do even more for you!

Jesus didn't say you should forget about the things that concern you. He said you have no need to panic. Don't allow those things to have a negative impact on you. ∎

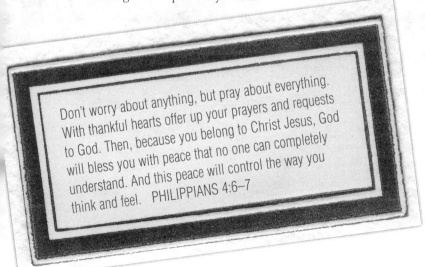

Don't worry about anything, but pray about everything. With thankful hearts offer up your prayers and requests to God. Then, because you belong to Christ Jesus, God will bless you with peace that no one can completely understand. And this peace will control the way you think and feel. PHILIPPIANS 4:6–7

Here are a few ideas for reducing the stress and worry in your life.

Pray as often as you need to—and then some.
Let the One who takes care of the birds and flowers of this world assist you too.

Do what you can do today.
If you have conflict or unresolved issues with someone, talk it out right away. If you have a looming deadline, do enough today to maintain your schedule.

Repeat the process tomorrow.
Learning to live one day at a time has changed the lives of countless broken and struggling people. Discover why for yourself.

Surround yourself with positive-thinking, calm people.
Pay attention to how they react to stressful situations and follow their example.

love (luv) a strong, deep, affection and devotion for another, unconditional and unexplain

6 Judge Not

There's an old saying that goes like this: "If you're being chased by a bear, you don't have to be the fastest person in your group; you just have to be faster than one other person."

That same mind-set lies at the heart of our judgmental tendencies. When we're being judged by others, we reason that we don't have to be better than everyone else. We just have to be better than one other person. So we find someone who seems worse than us and point our fingers.

Jesus revealed the faulty reasoning behind that attitude. He said, "Don't condemn others, and God won't condemn you. God will be as hard on you as you are on others! He will treat you exactly as you treat them" (Matthew 7:1–2).

Judging others actually puts us in God's crosshairs. Instead of condemning and looking down on people for their faults, a better alternative is praying for them and asking God to help them recognize their need to change. ■

7 Maintain an Outward Focus

The essence of genuine love is an outward focus, an emphasis on others instead of on ourselves. That would seem to be obvious. Yet many of us are tripped up by occasional inward glances. Our desire to promote ourselves—to make sure we aren't overlooked—obscures our focus on others.

That's why the apostle Paul felt the need to offer this reminder from 1 Corinthians 13:4:

"LOVE IS . . . NEVER . . . BOASTFUL."

To love someone is to

- CELEBRATE THE PERSON;
- IDENTIFY THE TRAITS THAT MAKE THE PERSON SPECIAL;
- DEVELOP A SENSE OF PRIDE IN BEING ASSOCIATED WITH THE PERSON;
- BE THANKFUL FOR THE PERSON'S PRESENCE IN YOUR LIFE.

In order to show the kind of love Paul was talking about, we must keep our focus on the other person. We must willingly risk being overlooked in the process. ■

Swallow Your Pride— Daily, If Necessary

"Love is . . . never . . . proud" (1 Corinthians 13:4).

8

The apostle Paul's reasoning is obvious. If our hearts are filled with self-regard, there's little room for love. What we need, then, is a way to keep our pride in check while we demonstrate our love for others.

The solution? Make a habit of recognizing and acknowledging other people's contributions to our lives.

There's no such thing as solitary stardom. Behind every successful person is a team of people who helped to make that success possible. If you've achieved success, no doubt there are others who have

- made sacrifices for you;
- worked alongside you;
- encouraged you;
- inspired you;
- given you opportunities;
- helped you mature.

You have the choice to celebrate yourself—to luxuriate in pride—or to acknowledge, regularly and sincerely, the contributions of others. For the sake of love, choose wisely. ∎

Love is patient and kind, never jealous, boastful, proud, or rude.

Make Your Love Fail-Safe

The apostle Paul wrapped up his examination of love in 1 Corinthians 13 with an audacious three-word claim: "Love never fails!"

(1 Corinthians 13:8).

The deepest kind of love is not based on emotions. It does not ebb and flow in the wake of petty annoyances or temporary changes of heart. It is not susceptible to the ravages of time. It is not weakened by outside forces. It is not put in limbo by separation. It does not fade into memory. It has no hidden agenda.

The love Paul talked about is always active, always fresh. It is rock solid, able to be counted on. It is a choice, an act of will. It is self-sacrificing, concerned more about the other person than about self. It comforts and it challenges. It is life changing. It is unforgettable.

It is made possible by Jesus' unfailing love for us. ■

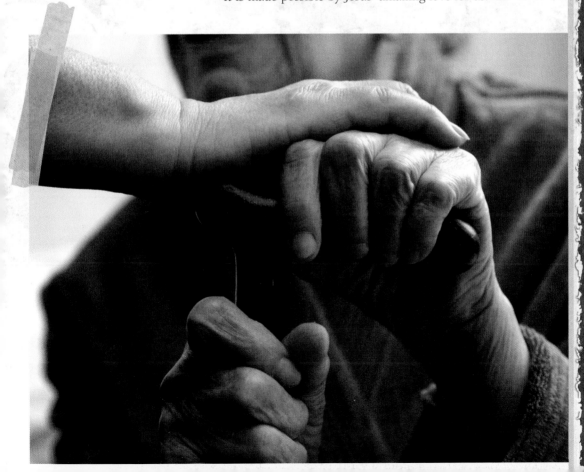

Because I love you

"I picked up a man from the street, and he was eaten up alive from worms. Nobody could stand him, and he was smelling so badly. I went to him to clean him, and he asked, 'Why do you do this?' I said, 'Because I love you.'"

Mother Teresa

Embrace Truth

10

"Love rejoices in the truth" (1 Corinthians 13:6).

Honesty is essential to every loving, healthy relationship. In fact, where truth is absent, a functional relationship cannot exist. If you've been on the receiving end of a particularly devastating lie, you know the effect it can have.

The problem is that truth can be difficult. Depending on the circumstances, lying often seems like the easier, more convenient, less messy, or even kinder option. So how can we keep a proper perspective toward the truth?

Below are a few suggestions for how you can make honesty a priority in your life.

SET THE BAR HIGH FOR YOURSELF.

You can't expect honesty from others if you don't offer it yourself, day in and day out. Work hard to establish (or maintain) a reputation for scrupulous—and loving—honesty. Make your word mean something. Keep in mind too that establishing a baseline of honesty in a relationship may require you to own up to past lies and set the record straight.

LEAVE NO DOUBT ABOUT WHERE YOU STAND ON THE MATTER.

Without being heavy handed, make sure people know you place a high priority on the truth. Don't confuse the issue by playing along or looking the other way when someone tells a "harmless" lie. Be consistent in your passion for the truth.

GIVE PEOPLE THE BENEFIT OF THE DOUBT . . . ONCE OR TWICE.

If you're not sure whether someone is telling the truth, err on the side of gullibility. If it turns out the person is being honest, you'll have avoided a potentially embarrassing situation. If it turns out the person is lying, repeat to yourself: "Fool me once, shame on you; fool me twice, shame on me."

RESPOND APPROPRIATELY WHEN PEOPLE DO TELL YOU THE TRUTH.

This is especially important if someone tells you an uncomfortable truth—one that you may not want to hear. Before you get into the specifics of the uncomfortable truth, make sure you acknowledge the courage it took to bring it to your attention. If you're going to be someone who rejoices in the truth, you need to accept truth in all its forms.

CONFRONT (IN A LOVING WAY) PEOPLE WHO LIE TO YOU.

Don't ignore untruths because you want to keep the peace. Bring them out into the open. Let people know how you feel. ■

Live with Eternity in Mind

If heaven is our ultimate destination, what does that mean for our time on earth? That's a question every follower of Jesus wrestles with.

In his letter to the Philippians, the apostle Paul weighed in on the subject. "But we are citizens of heaven and are eagerly waiting for our Savior to come from there" (Philippians 3:20).

As "citizens of heaven," followers of Jesus may—and should—feel out of place in this world. The Bible promises that something unimaginably good is waiting for us beyond this life. That promise, when properly understood, makes earthly excitements and priorities pale in comparison. It puts earthly problems in their proper context and helps us see them as mere blips in the whole scheme of eternity. And it makes our earthly pain and suffering a little more bearable, since we recognize that it's all temporary. ■

THE BEAUTY OF HEAVEN

"We may speak about a place where there are no tears, no death, no fear, no night; but those are just the benefits of heaven. The beauty of heaven is seeing God."

Max Lucado, *Experiencing the Heart of Jesus Workbook: Knowing His Heart, Feeling His Love*

11

But we are citizens of heaven and are eagerly waiting for our Savior to come from there.

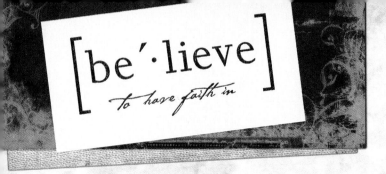

[be´·lieve]
to have faith in

Be Awed Every Day 12

God once described David as "the kind of person who pleases me most" (Acts 13:22).

When you read some of David's writings in the book of Psalms, it's easy to see why. Take, for example, David's words in Psalm 8:3–4: "I often think of the heavens your hands have made, and of the moon and stars you put in place. Then I ask, 'Why do you care about us humans? Why are you concerned for us weaklings?' "

David never lost his sense of awe at the world around him. He looked deep into the night sky and marveled at the fact that its Designer cared about him.

Do you share David's sense of awe? Do you spend time contemplating and appreciating the world around you? Do you maintain an attitude of humility and gratitude? Are you the kind of person who pleases God most? ■

Find the Silver Lining in Everything 13

"My friends, be glad, even if you have a lot of trouble. You know you learn to endure by having your faith tested. But you must learn to endure everything, so you will be completely mature and not lacking in anything" (James 1:2–4).

How is it possible to be glad in times of trouble? By reminding yourself that there's something to be gained from every loss, every failure, and every setback—if you look for it.

Enduring trouble and pain gives us a perspective and maturity we can't get any other way. Our hard-earned life experiences make us more mature—and more empathetic to other hurting people.

You may not be ready to thank God for the trials and suffering in your life, but you can thank him for the results they produce in you. ■

Treat Money as a Tool, Not a Treasure

1 Timothy 6:10

14

The apostle Paul warned, "The love of money causes all kinds of trouble. Some people want money so much they have given up their faith and caused themselves a lot of pain" (1 Timothy 6:10).

That's a troubling thought—one that raises an important question. In a culture that worships the almighty dollar, how do we keep from falling in love with money?

First, we remember to thank God for everything we receive. By giving thanks, we acknowledge that the money didn't originate with us and ultimately is not ours.

Second, we cheerfully and willingly give back to God by donating to churches and to people in need. The Bible is full of examples of men and women who acknowledged God as the source of all they had and, in return, gave back a portion of what they had to him.

Third, we treat money as a tool, not a treasure. God gave it to us for a reason. We should use it in a way that honors him. ■

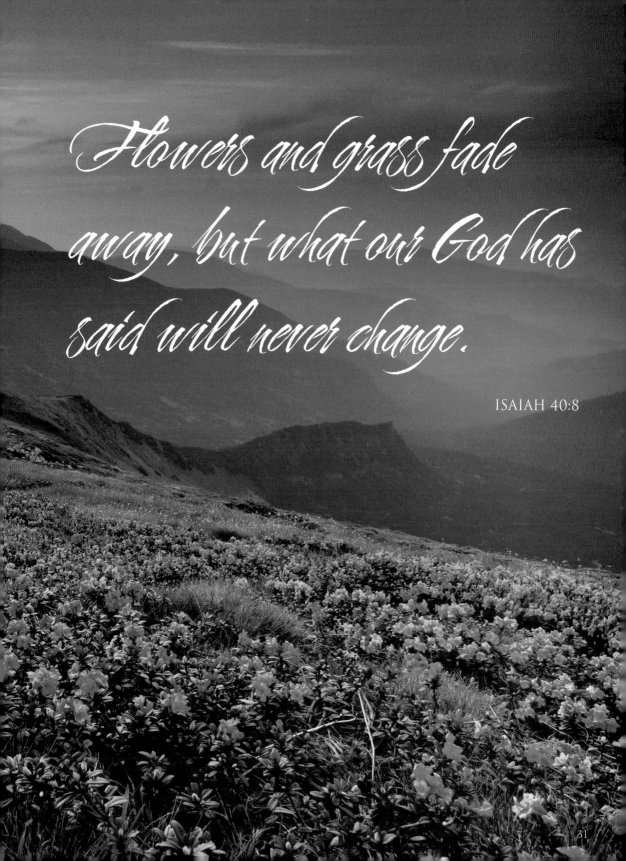

Flowers and grass fade away, but what our God has said will never change.

ISAIAH 40:8

31

Never Throw the First Stone

15

Wisdom
PSALM 25:6–8

Please, LORD, remember, you have always been patient and kind. Forget each wrong I did when I was young. Show how truly kind you are and remember me. You are honest and merciful, and you teach sinners how to follow your path.

The Pharisees (religious leaders) of Jesus' day believed his teachings were dangerous. They attempted on several occasions to corner Jesus into expressing his views to them clearly. One day they brought to him a woman who had been caught having an adulterous affair. They asked him if the woman should be stoned to death.

If Jesus had said no, he would have gone against Jewish law, which said that adultery should be punished by death. If he said yes, he would have gone against Roman law, which did not allow Jewish people to carry out their own executions.

Jesus said neither of those things. In fact, he said nothing at all for a while.

But Jesus simply bent over and started writing on the ground with his finger.

They kept on asking Jesus about the woman. Finally, he stood up and said, "If any of you have never sinned, then go ahead and throw the first stone at her!" Once again he bent over and began writing on the ground. The people left one by one, beginning with the oldest. Finally, Jesus and the woman were there alone.

Jesus stood up and asked her, "Where is everyone? Isn't there anyone left to accuse you?"

"No sir," the woman answered.

Then Jesus told her, "I am not going to accuse you either. You may go now, but don't sin anymore." (John 8:6–11)

We are all flawed, and none of us has lived an error-free life. We would do well to remember the words of Jesus in Luke 6:37: "Don't judge others, and God won't judge you." The next time you feel tempted to join a chorus of condemnation, try these alternatives.

Take a look at yourself.

Are there things in your life you could be condemned for? Have you dealt with them in the way you should?

Recognize that anyone can make a mistake.

Without excusing the person's wrongdoing, acknowledge that being human carries with it some serious liabilities, including being vulnerable to temptation. Think about the last temptation that tripped you up.

Talk to the person in private, if possible.

Instead of making your concerns public, go to the source. Find out if you have your facts straight. Get his or her side of the story. ∎

16 Choose Your Advisers Carefully

When Solomon succeeded his father, David, as king of Israel, God told the young monarch to ask for anything he wanted—fame, wealth, power—and it would be given to him. Solomon chose wisdom. He wanted the ability to make wise decisions as the ruler of Israel. God was so pleased with Solomon's answer that he made him wiser than anyone who's ever lived (and then threw in fame, wealth, and power to boot).

Solomon was known throughout the ancient world for his discernment—his ability to choose the best course of action in any situation. People from distant lands regularly traveled to Jerusalem just to witness his wisdom in action.

The book of Proverbs is Solomon's "how-to" manual—his primer on supernatural discernment. A key theme of Proverbs is finding the right sources of wisdom. Solomon described the search this way: "My child, you must follow and treasure my teachings and my instructions. Keep in tune with wisdom and think what it means to have common sense. Beg as loud as you can for good common sense. Search for wisdom as you would search for silver or hidden treasure. Then you will understand what it means to respect and to know the LORD God" (Proverbs 2:1–5).

To be wise, you must recognize and value the right instruction. In other words, you have to know where to look and whom to listen to. That's the challenge.

One thing is certain, though: you'll find no shortage of would-be advisers jockeying for your attention. Everyone has advice to offer, life experiences to pass along, instructions for doing things the right way, and rules to live by. The question is, which ones should you take to heart?

In order to give your search for wisdom due diligence, as Solomon recommended, you need to carefully evaluate the people who advise you.

- Do they have a good reputation? Is their integrity apparent? Are they trustworthy? Are they respected by people you respect?

- Does their advice jibe with that of other people you trust? Does it depart radically from an accepted body of wisdom?

- Do they practice what they preach? Has their philosophy and outlook made a difference in their own lives?

You only get one chance at this life. Surround yourself with the best people. Choose your advisers wisely. ■

THE STRENGTH OF
Wisdom

ECCLESIASTES 7:15-29

I have seen everything during this senseless life of mine. I have seen good citizens die for doing the right thing, while criminals live and prosper. So don't destroy yourself by being too good or acting too smart! Don't die before your time by being too evil or acting like a fool. Keep to the middle of the road. You can do this if you truly respect God.

Wisdom will make you stronger than the ten most powerful leaders in your city.

No one in this world always does right.

Don't listen to everything that everyone says, or you might hear your servant cursing you. Haven't you cursed many others?

I told myself that I would be smart and try to understand all this, but it was too much for me. The truth is beyond us. It's far too deep. So I decided to learn everything I could and become wise enough to discover what life is all about. At the same time, I wanted to understand why it's stupid and senseless to be an evil fool.

. . . With all my wisdom I have tried to find out how everything fits together, but so far I have not been able to. . . . I did learn one thing: We were completely honest when God created us, but now we have twisted minds.

I AM THE VINE, AND YOU ARE THE BRANCHES. IF YOU STAY JOINED TO ME, AND I STAY JOINED TO YOU, THEN YOU WILL PRODUCE LOTS OF FRUIT. BUT YOU CANNOT DO ANYTHING WITHOUT ME.

JOHN 15:5

17

Keep Hope Alive

In Romans 5, the apostle Paul addressed first-century Christians who were being persecuted because of their faith. Paul urged the struggling believers to embrace their suffering.

In Romans 5:4, he revealed the endgame: "Endurance builds character, which gives us a hope." Enduring suffering ultimately leads to hope. In this case, though, hope isn't wishful thinking; it's confidence in God.

Think of it as a spiritual variation of "Whatever doesn't kill you makes you stronger." When we endure a painful experience and come out the other side, we get a better understanding of what God is capable of. Thus, when the next crisis arises, we have a stronger confidence and deeper sense of hope in him. ■

Wisdom

ROMANS 5:1–5

By faith we have been made acceptable to God. And now, thanks to our Lord Jesus Christ, we have peace with God. Christ has also introduced us to God's gift of undeserved grace on which we now take our stand. So we are happy, as we look forward to sharing in the glory of God. But that's not all! We gladly suffer, because we know that suffering helps us to endure. And endurance builds character, which gives us a hope that will never disappoint us. All of this happens because God has given us the Holy Spirit, who fills our hearts with his love.

Enjoy God's Presence

God gives us salvation through his Son, Jesus.
That's the central theme of Christianity.

With the gift of salvation, however, comes something equally valuable. The apostle John describes it this way: "God has given us his Spirit. This is how we know we are one with him, just as he is one with us" (1 John 4:13).

How do we know we belong to God? We have his Spirit inside us. We have access to his strength when we're tempted. We have access to his guidance when we're lost. We have access to his wisdom when we're confused. We have a direct line to him when we need to talk. If we think it, he hears it; when we ask questions, he answers us.

How often do we thank God for such an incredible gift? How often do we take advantage of the opportunities the Holy Spirit offers? ■

Light the Way

for Others 19

Jesus referred to himself as "the light for the world" (John 8:12). A light capable of illuminating the entire world is obviously very powerful—so powerful, in fact, that it is reflected off anything or anyone close to it. Just as the moon reflects the sun's light, followers of Jesus reflect his light by showing love and compassion to other people.

Jesus made that clear in his first sermon to his followers. He stated: "You are the light for the whole world. A city built on top of a hill cannot be hidden, and no one lights a lamp and puts it under a clay pot. Instead, it is placed on a lampstand, where it can give light to everyone in the house. Make your light shine, so others will see the good you do and will praise your Father in heaven" (Matthew 5:14–16).

We have the choice of letting our lights shine or covering them up. Jesus urged us to switch on our high beams and let them brightly blaze so that others will see them and be drawn to him.

Sounds simple, but many people would prefer to keep their lights hidden—or at least partially hidden. The pressure of standing out so obviously from the crowd is too much. So they hide their lights by keeping quiet when they should speak up, by following the crowd instead of leading the way.

If you're ever tempted to dim your light, think about who may suffer as a result. How many friends, family members, coworkers, neighbors, teammates, and acquaintances look to you for direction—perhaps without your even knowing? How many hurting people draw comfort from you? How many directionless people now find their way, thanks to you? How will the people you care about be affected if they can't count on your light?

When people see a difference—marked by love and kindness—in the way you live your life, they're not looking at *your* light. They're looking at Jesus' light. The question is, will you allow that light to shine in your life? ■

20 Don't Be a Stranger to God

Around 874 BC, the nation of Judah was under siege by Israel. Israel had the upper hand in the conflict because of its alliance with the powerful nation of Aram. Asa, the king of Judah, devised a strategy for turning the tables on Israel. He emptied all the gold and silver from his palace and the temple and sent it to the king of Aram. His message was simple: "I'm giving you all this silver and gold as a gift. Now, please break your treaty with Israel."

Asa's plan worked. Aram broke its treaty with Israel, forcing the Israelites to retreat. Judah was saved—or so Asa thought. That's when a prophet named Hanani showed up with a message: "The LORD is constantly watching everyone, and he gives strength to those who faithfully obey him. But you have done a foolish thing, and your kingdom will never be at peace again" (2 Chronicles 16:9). God was unhappy with Asa for going to the king of Aram—instead of to God—for help. As punishment, Judah would remain at war for as long as Asa was king.

Asa had managed to engineer his own solution. What was so wrong with that?

We live in an age when self-reliance of the sort Asa displayed is valued. We feel pressured to have all the answers. But the reality is, we don't. Our horizons are more limited than we often care to admit. Turning to a higher power can help put our egos back into perspective.

King Asa had no real defense against Hanani's accusation. Do we? After all, we have access to God every day too. So why not take advantage of it? The Bible makes it clear that God is always available to anyone who seeks him. So why don't we seek God more? Why do we too often remain strangers? ∎

King Asa of Judah Destroying the Idols. Oil on canvas.
François de Nomé © Fitzwilliam Museum, Cambridge / Art Resource, NY

More to the point, how do we initiate a closer relationship with God? Here are tips to get you started.

Find a place where you can focus on God.

The ideal location would be someplace quiet and private—perhaps even a little isolated—where God's handiwork is on display. Local parks, hiking trails, and walking paths would be great places to start. Wherever you choose, make sure you free yourself from interruptions while you're there. Turn off your communication devices.

Learn as much as you can about God from people who knew him well.

Everything God wants us to know about him can be found in the Bible. Read it to

- get a sense of the things God has done;
- find out how God has interacted with different people;
- discover clues as to what God likes and dislikes—anything that might help develop your own relationship with God.

Keep your conversations fresh and interesting.

Pray often—and creatively. Don't settle for standard prayers or words you think you're supposed to say. Talk to God like you would to a friend—the greatest friend ever.

"The Christian who is truly intimate with Jesus will never draw attention to himself but will only show the evidence of a life where Jesus is completely in control. This is the outcome of allowing Jesus to satisfy every area of life to its depth. The picture resulting from such a life is that of the strong, calm balance that our Lord gives to those who are intimate with Him."

Oswald Chambers, *My Utmost for His Highest*

Choose Hope

Jesus was in Perea when he received word that Lazarus, one of his close friends, was sick. (Lazarus was the brother of Mary and Martha, two of Jesus' most devoted followers.) Rather than rush to Bethany to be with Lazarus, Jesus tarried in Perea for two more days. And then he began his journey.

By the time Jesus arrived in Bethany, Lazarus was dead. His body had been in the tomb for four days. Mary and Martha were understandably beside themselves with grief.

"Martha said to Jesus, 'Lord, if you had been here, my brother would not have died.' . . . Jesus then said, 'I am the one who raises the dead to life! Everyone who has faith in me will live, even if they die' " (John 11:21, 25).

Jesus knew he was going to raise Lazarus from the dead, but Mary and Martha didn't. Their grief was real. Their emotions were raw. Jesus wasn't upset by their reaction—he'd cried too—but he wanted to help them through their pain to get to something better: *hope*.

That journey from devastation to hope can be plotted by boiling Jesus' words down to these three words: *Believe in me*.

Don't give grief and pain the final word. Believe in me.

Don't let your world come crashing down around you. Believe in me.

Don't give up. Believe in me.

All it takes is one tragedy—one unexpected loss—to drive home the point that we are practically powerless to control or prevent the things that happen to us. The one area we can control, however, is how we will respond. We can choose devastation and surrender—or we can choose hope and perseverance.

To choose hope and perseverance is not to brush aside our grief. It is to address our pain head-on and to work through our feelings (with the assistance of a professional counselor, if necessary). To choose hope is to believe that happiness and joy are attainable again, despite what our grief tells us.

To choose hope is to take Jesus at his word when he says, *Believe in me. I am more powerful than your pain. I will carry you through. I will heal your heart.* ■

21

"HOPE IS A
WAKING DREAM."
Augustine

Beyond Beauty

Most people, if they had really learned to look into their own hearts, would know that they do want, and want acutely, something that cannot be had in this world. There are all sorts of things in this world that offer to give it to you, but they never quite keep their promise.

At present we are on the outside . . . the wrong side of the door. We discern the freshness and purity of morning, but they do not make us fresh and pure. We cannot mingle with the pleasures we see. But all the pages of the New Testament are rustling with the rumor that it will not always be so. Someday, God willing, we shall get "in" . . . We will put on glory . . . that greater glory of which Nature is only the first sketch.

We do not want to merely "see" beauty—though, God knows, even that is bounty enough. We want something else which can hardly be put into words—to be united with the beauty we see, to pass into it, to receive it into ourselves, to bathe in it, to become part of it.

C. S. LEWIS

Keep Your Books Balanced

22

Debt reduction is a timely topic—and has been for at least 2,000 years, judging from the apostle Paul's words in Romans 13:7–8: "Pay all that you owe, whether it is taxes and fees or respect and honor. Let love be your only debt! If you love others, you have done all that the Law demands."

You'll notice that Paul took the discussion out of the realm of the fiscal almost immediately. This isn't just about financial bookkeeping. It's about living with integrity. This is about enjoying healthy relationships and maintaining balance in our lives.

Paul pointed out that our debts may include respect and honor. That means if there are people in our lives who deserve (or prefer) to be treated with an extra measure of courtesy or deference—because of their age, position, or background—we should oblige. Likewise, if we know people who warrant special recognition for things they've accomplished, we should offer that as well. Fulfilling such obligations not only benefits others but is also good for us. It moves us closer to being debt free. ■

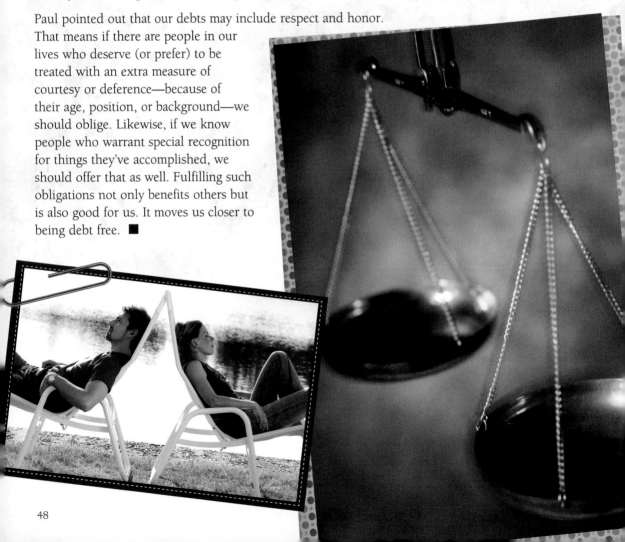

Here are a few other ideas that might fall under Paul's heading of debt reduction.

IF YOU OWE A PHONE CALL, YOU SHOULD MAKE IT.

If you've lost touch with a friend, it's time to reestablish the connection.

IF YOU OWE AN EXPLANATION, YOU SHOULD OFFER IT.

If someone somewhere is wondering why you did something, it's time to explain yourself.

IF YOU OWE AN APOLOGY, YOU SHOULD MAKE IT.

If you've wronged someone, it's time to seek forgiveness and make things right.

IF YOU OWE GRATITUDE, YOU SHOULD GIVE IT.

It's time to let the people who've made a difference in your life know how thankful you are.

IF YOU OWE YOUR TIME AND ATTENTION, YOU SHOULD OFFER THEM.

If you claim that someone or something is a priority, it's time to show it.

IF YOU OWE A CONFRONTATION, YOU SHOULD INITIATE IT.

If you've let a problem situation go, it's time to address it.

IF YOU OWE DISCIPLINE, YOU SHOULD GIVE IT.

If you've skirted your duties as a parent or manager, it's time to make amends.

The more unpaid debts you're able to settle, the more balance you'll restore to your life.

GOD BLESSES THOSE PEOPLE...

MATTHEW 5:3–10

...WHO DEPEND ONLY ON HIM.
They belong to the kingdom of heaven!

...WHO GRIEVE.
They will find comfort!

...WHO ARE HUMBLE.
The earth will belong to them!

...WHO WANT TO OBEY HIM MORE THAN TO EAT OR DRINK.
They will be given what they want!

...WHO ARE MERCIFUL.
They will be treated with mercy!

...WHOSE HEARTS ARE PURE.
They will see him!

...WHO MAKE PEACE.
They will be called his children!

...WHO ARE TREATED BADLY FOR DOING RIGHT.
They belong to the kingdom of heaven.

The Sermon of the Beatitudes, 1886–1896
James Tissot (1836–1902)

Don't Look for Deep Fulfillment in Shallow Things

23

What do you get for the man who has everything? Judging by Solomon's words in Ecclesiastes 2:1–11, you give him a sense of purpose or meaning.

I said to myself, "Have fun and enjoy yourself!" But this didn't make sense. Laughing and having fun is crazy. What good does it do? I wanted to find out what was best for us during the short time we have on this earth. So I decided to make myself happy with wine and find out what it means to be foolish, without really being foolish myself.

I did some great things. I built houses and planted vineyards. I had flower gardens and orchards full of fruit trees. And I had pools where I could get water for the trees. I owned slaves, and their sons and daughters became my slaves. I had more sheep and goats than anyone who had ever lived in Jerusalem. Foreign rulers brought me silver, gold, and precious treasures. Men and women sang for me, and I had many wives who gave me great pleasure.

I was the most famous person who had ever lived in Jerusalem, and I was very wise. I got whatever I wanted and did whatever made me happy. But most of all, I enjoyed my work. Then I thought about everything I had done, including the hard work, and it was simply chasing the wind. Nothing on earth is worth the trouble.

On the surface, Solomon was recalling a life well lived—perhaps the most enviable existence of them all. Beneath the celebration, though, lay despair and hopelessness—and one of Solomon's hardest-earned lessons: all the pleasures, possessions, and accomplishments in the world cannot bring fulfillment. Solomon experimented with nearly everything, and he found meaning in none of it. ■

In truth, deep fulfillment cannot be found in shallow pleasures. Fulfillment springs from things that matter, things that have an impact not just on yourself but on others as well. Fulfillment is found in the following things:

Healthy relationships

It comes from investing yourself in others and allowing them to do the same for you.

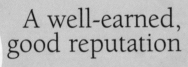

A well-earned, good reputation

It comes from being quietly recognized as one who lives a life of integrity and loving concern for others.

Spiritual peace

It comes from having an obstacle-free relationship with God.

YOU CANNOT SERVE GOD AND MONEY

Jesus Tells the Parable of the Unjust Steward

Jesus said to his disciples:

A rich man once had a manager to take care of his business. But he was told that his manager was wasting money. So the rich man called him in and said, "What is this I hear about you? Tell me what you have done! You are no longer going to work for me."

The manager said to himself, "What shall I do now that my master is going to fire me? I can't dig ditches, and I'm ashamed to beg. I know what I'll do, so that people will welcome me into their homes after I've lost my job."

Then one by one he called in the people who were in debt to his master. He asked the first one, "How much do you owe my master?"

"A hundred barrels of olive oil," the man answered.

So the manager said, "Take your bill and sit down and quickly write '50.' "

The manager asked someone else who was in debt to his master, "How much do you owe?"

"A thousand sacks of wheat," the man replied.

The manager said, "Take your bill and write '800.' "

The master praised his dishonest manager for looking out for himself so well. That's how it is! The people of this world look out for themselves better than the people who belong to the light.

My disciples, I tell you to use wicked wealth to make friends for yourselves. Then when it is gone, you will be welcomed into an eternal home. Anyone who can be trusted in little matters can also be trusted in important matters. But anyone who is dishonest in little matters will be dishonest in important matters. If you cannot be trusted with this wicked wealth, who will trust you with true wealth? And if you cannot be trusted with what belongs to someone else, who will give you something that will be your own? You cannot be the slave of two masters. You will like one more than the other or be more loyal to one than to the other. You cannot serve God and money.

Luke 16:1–13

GOD INTENDED MONEY TO HELP OTHERS

Jesus Tells a Story of Lazarus and the Rich Man

There was once a rich man who wore expensive clothes and every day ate the best food. But a poor beggar named Lazarus was brought to the gate of the rich man's house. He was happy just to eat the scraps that fell from the rich man's table. His body was covered with sores, and dogs kept coming up to lick them. The poor man died, and angels took him to the place of honor next to Abraham.

The rich man also died and was buried. He went to hell and was suffering terribly. When he looked up and saw Abraham far off and Lazarus at his side, he said to Abraham, "Have pity on me! Send Lazarus to dip his finger in water and touch my tongue. I'm suffering terribly in this fire."

Abraham answered, "My friend, remember that while you lived, you had everything good, and Lazarus had everything bad. Now he is happy, and you are in pain. And besides, there is a deep ditch between us, and no one from either side can cross over."

But the rich man said, "Abraham, then please send Lazarus to my father's home. Let him warn my five brothers, so they won't come to this horrible place."

Abraham answered, "Your brothers can read what Moses and the prophets wrote. They should pay attention to that."

Then the rich man said, "No, that's not enough! If only someone from the dead would go to them, they would listen and turn to God."

So Abraham said, "If they won't pay attention to Moses and the prophets, they won't listen even to someone who comes back from the dead."

Luke 16:19–31

Lazarus at the Rich Man's Gate, 1886
Fyodor Bronnikov

Keep Your Nostalgia in Check

24

The temptation to look back on our formative years through rose-colored glasses is hard to resist. After all, people were kinder/smarter/friendlier/thriftier/better dressed/more respectful of their elders back then. The world was simpler. You could get more for a dollar. The entertainment choices were better. Life was easier.

Or so we would like to believe.

That tendency to glorify the past—to rhapsodize over what used to be—is nothing new. The adults of 720 BC likely believed that life was much better back in the 750s and 740s BC. The people of 1000 BC probably longed for the good old days of 1125 BC.

Such nostalgia may seem like a harmless pastime, but the writer of Ecclesiastes had a different take: "It isn't wise to ask, 'Why is everything worse than it used to be?' " (Ecclesiastes 7:10).

He recognized that nostalgia is often a reaction to troubling current situations—a retreat from the problems of today. Putting the previous decade or two on a pedestal does nothing to help us address the issues of the here and now.

That's not to say the past is useless to us. As George Santayana famously noted, "Those who cannot remember the past are condemned to repeat it." The key word in that quote is *remember*. And that's where nostalgia often falls short.

The truth is, the good old days weren't always so good. We tend to gloss over things that don't conform to our rosy hindsight. And in the process, we lose sight of many areas in which our society has improved. We can learn from the past only if we can recall it clearly and objectively.

A better strategy is to save nostalgia for birthdays, anniversaries, reunions, and scrapbooks. Leave the past in the past. Instead of resting on your laurels, blaze a new trail. Today, tomorrow, and the days that lie ahead are where your focus should be. That's where the fulfillment of your potential resides.

In other words, don't look back. ■

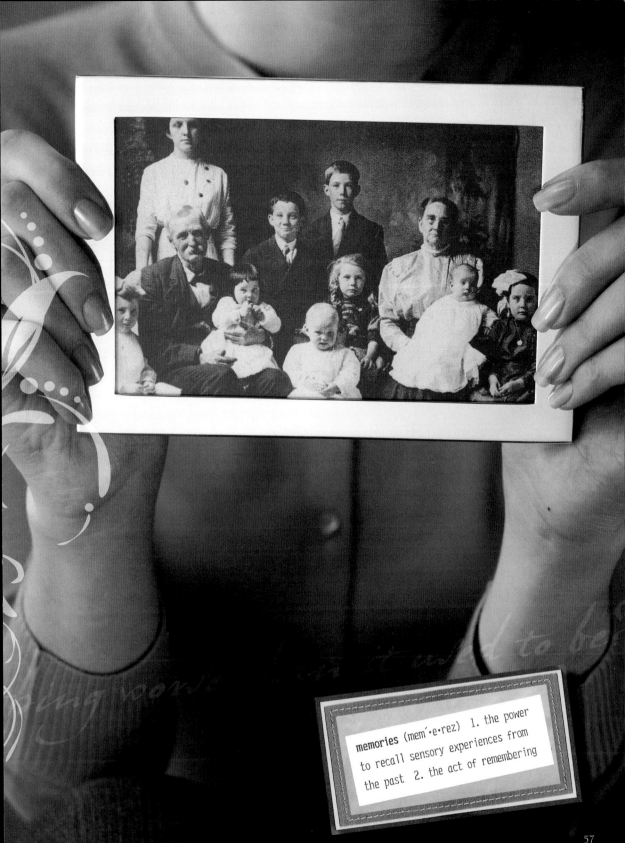

memories (mem´·e·rez) 1. the power to recall sensory experiences from the past 2. the act of remembering

57

25

Be a Stealthy Giver

Every year some entertainment magazine or nonprofit organization makes a list of the most generous celebrities in Hollywood— the stars who give the most money to charity. The list is compiled based on information supplied by the celebrities themselves (through their publicists, of course). It seems no one in Hollywood can make a contribution without calling a press conference to announce it.

As far as Jesus is concerned, their generosity is compromised. These are his words:

> When you do good deeds, don't try to show off. If you do, you won't get a reward from your Father in heaven.
>
> When you give to the poor, don't blow a loud horn. That's what show-offs do in the synagogues and on the street corners, because they are always looking for praise. I can assure you that they already have their reward.
>
> When you give to the poor, don't let anyone know about it. Then your gift will be given in secret. Your Father knows what is done in secret and will reward you. (Matthew 6:1–4)

If you want to give in a way that pleases God, here's what to do:

Don't advertise it.

Resist the urge to promote yourself or call attention to your generosity. No one needs to know how much you've given—not even the people you're assisting. That should be between you and God.

Cut all strings to it.

When you give to others, you pass on what God has given to you. If you try to benefit from a gift you offer—or place any conditions on it—it ceases to be a gift and starts to become a bribe.

Forget about it.

There are three steps to the giving process:

Step 1 – Give the gift quietly.
Step 2 – Thank God for allowing you to give.
Step 3 – Move on.

Dwelling on your generosity can lead to excessive pride—and nothing good comes from that.

Maintain a proper perspective.

No matter how generous you are, you still receive infinitely more from God than you give to others. No one outgives God. That's why humility must always run hand in hand with generosity. ∎

2 CORINTHIANS 9:6–15

Remember this saying,

"A few seeds make a small harvest,
but a lot of seeds make a big harvest."

Each of you must make up your own mind about how much to
give. But don't feel sorry that you must give and don't feel you
are forced to give. God loves people who love to give. God can
bless you with everything you need, and you will always have
more than enough to do all kinds of good things for others.

The Scriptures say,
"God freely gives his gifts to the poor, and always does right."

God gives seed to farmers and provides everyone with food. He
will increase what you have, so that you can give even more to
those in need. You will be blessed in every way, and you will be
able to keep on being generous. Then many people will thank
God when we deliver your gift.

What you are doing is much more than a service that supplies
God's people with what they need. It is something that will make
many others thank God. The way in which you have proved
yourselves by this service will bring honor and praise to God.
You believed the message about Christ, and you obeyed it by
sharing generously with God's people and with everyone else.
Now they are praying for you and want to see you, because God
used you to bless them so very much. Thank God for his gift
that is too wonderful for words!

Pay Your Taxes

Bring up the topic of taxes with a group of people and you are likely to ignite a heated debate. Are you paying your fair share? Should the government tax you more or less?

Jesus' perspective on taxes may surprise you. When he lived on earth, Jesus was a citizen of the Roman Empire. Ironically, he would have been responsible to pay taxes that funded the government that eventually gave him an unjust trial and death sentence.

Even though Jesus knew the role the Roman government would ultimately play in his own suffering, he did not advise anyone to opt out of paying their taxes. Instead, he encouraged people to pay their taxes without a second thought. He said, *"Give the Emperor what belongs to him and give God what belongs to God"* (Matthew 22:21). How could Jesus commend paying taxes to a corrupt government? How could he support a legal system that supported torture and crucifixion? The answer lies in Jesus' perspective.

Christ's eyes were focused on a different kingdom. He was focused on God and his work and did not find his true home here on earth. His true home was heaven, and he encouraged his followers to have the same perspective by giving to "God what belongs to God."

If we aim to follow God and focus our hearts on heaven, then mundane and earthly duties (like paying taxes) can become less of a frustrating burden. ∎

Wisdom

MATTHEW 17:24–27

When Jesus and the others arrived in Capernaum, the collectors for the temple tax came to Peter and asked, "Does your teacher pay the temple tax?"

"Yes, he does," Peter answered. . . .

. . . [Later Jesus said to Peter], "We don't want to cause trouble. So go cast a line into the lake and pull out the first fish you hook. Open its mouth, and you will find a coin. Use it to pay your taxes and mine."

Recognize Evil for What It Is

27

In the apostle Paul's far-reaching examination of love in 1 Corinthians 13, he touched on the subject of good and evil. Specifically, he said, "Love rejoices in the truth, but not in evil" (1 Corinthians 13:6).

At first glance, the topic seems out of place. After all, what does evil have to do with love? However, when you look at it in terms of addiction, self-harm, or personal demons, the connection makes sense. Anything people do to hurt themselves or others could rightly be called "evil"—the opposite of good.

Too often, though, well-meaning people turn a blind eye to such evil—in the name of love. They overlook things that should not be overlooked so as not to hurt, embarrass, or upset a loved one. They may not be rejoicing in evil, but they are allowing it to continue. And that fits no one's definition of love.

The kind of love Paul described in 1 Corinthians 13 actively opposes evil. Those who embody this type of love take action against evil in the lives of their loved ones. Taking this type of decisive action may not be easy.

The first step is to work up the courage to call something evil (being careful not to give our loved ones the impression that we're calling them evil). We acknowledge that whatever is hurting our loved ones—or causing them to hurt others—is wrong. That may be difficult, especially if we're used to looking the other way or making excuses for our loved ones.

When you take this first step, your loved one may not understand your new attitude—and may even be offended by it—but that's a risk you must take. As philosopher Edmund Burke (presumably) wrote, "The only thing necessary for the triumph of evil is that good men should do nothing."

> **ROMANS 13:12**
> Night is almost over, and day will soon appear. We must stop behaving as people do in the dark and be ready to live in the light.

Once you've made your feelings known in a firm but loving way, the ball is in your loved one's court. You can't forcibly remove evil from others' lives. They have to make the choice to remove it themselves—especially where addiction is involved.

You can, however, commit yourself to walking alongside your loved one throughout the process. You can offer your help and make yourself available when you're needed.

The kind of love Paul described in 1 Corinthians 13 doesn't come easily or naturally. It requires courage, commitment, and a willingness to fight for others. Are you up to the challenge? ■

63

28

Embrace Your Weakness

The apostle Paul suffered from some sort of physical ailment. Some have suggested that it was a disease of the eyes. Others think it was malaria or epilepsy. The Bible doesn't specify what the problem was, only that it was a chronic and debilitating condition that sometimes kept Paul from working.

More than once, Paul prayed about his problem. Here's how Paul described the encounters: "Three times I begged the Lord to make this suffering go away. But he replied, 'My gift of undeserved grace is all you need. My power is strongest when you are weak.' So if Christ keeps giving me his power, I will gladly brag about how weak I am. Yes, I am glad to be weak or insulted or mistreated or to have troubles and sufferings, if it is for Christ. Because when I am weak, I am strong" (2 Corinthians 12:8–10).

God heard Paul's intense pleas for healing . . . and said no. Paul was useful to him just the way he was.

For one thing, Paul's weakness made him a more effective leader. When God chose not to relieve him of his physical condition, Paul accepted the response with grace and gratitude. His faith didn't waver. The people who looked to him for guidance likely found strength to accept their own shortcomings and afflictions, based on Paul's response.

Paul's weakness also allowed him to empathize with other hurting people. When he talked to those who were suffering, he didn't have to imagine how they were feeling. He knew from firsthand experience. He understood their pain, their frustration, their desperation, their doubts, and their tough questions for God.

Our weaknesses should spur our empathy as well. It's one thing to feel sorry for hurting people; it's quite another to share common ground with them and truly understand what they're feeling and what they need.

Ultimately, Paul's affliction kept him humble. The apostle was, by nature, a self-sufficient man. His physical weakness forced him to confront his vulnerability and powerlessness. It reminded him of his constant need for God. Our weaknesses can do the same for us. ■

> "True contentment is a real, even an active, virtue—not only affirmative but creative. It is the power of getting out of any situation all there is in it."
>
> G. K. Chesterton

PSALM 104:24-28

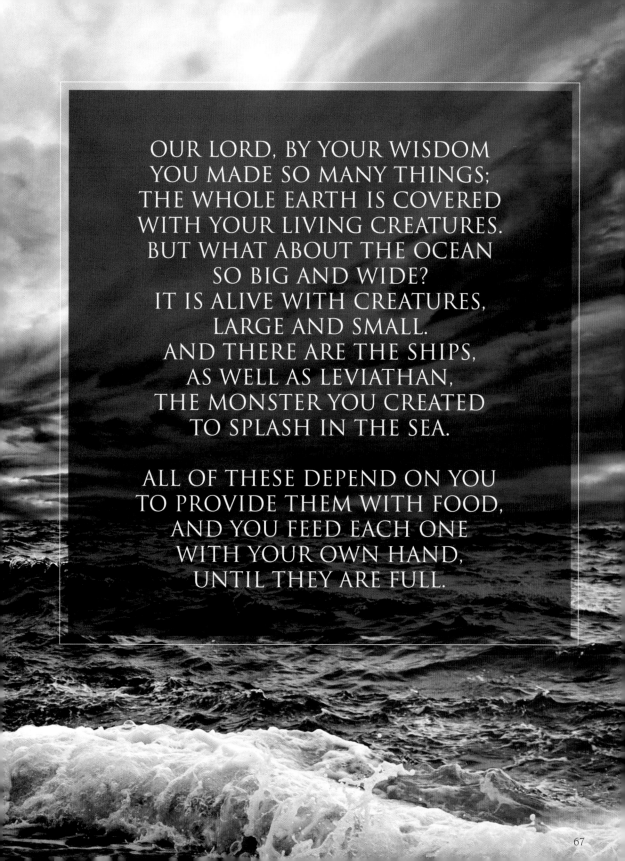

OUR LORD, BY YOUR WISDOM
YOU MADE SO MANY THINGS;
THE WHOLE EARTH IS COVERED
WITH YOUR LIVING CREATURES.
BUT WHAT ABOUT THE OCEAN
SO BIG AND WIDE?
IT IS ALIVE WITH CREATURES,
LARGE AND SMALL.
AND THERE ARE THE SHIPS,
AS WELL AS LEVIATHAN,
THE MONSTER YOU CREATED
TO SPLASH IN THE SEA.

ALL OF THESE DEPEND ON YOU
TO PROVIDE THEM WITH FOOD,
AND YOU FEED EACH ONE
WITH YOUR OWN HAND,
UNTIL THEY ARE FULL.

Know When to Let Others Help

29

The do-it-yourself mentality runs deep in our culture. We prize independence and celebrate people who take care of themselves and others. The apostle Paul, however, challenged that mind-set in his letter to the Galatians: "You obey the law of Christ when you offer each other a helping hand" (Galatians 6:2).

For many people, the most difficult part of this instruction is contained in the words "each other," which suggest a give-and-take arrangement—sometimes we're the helpers and sometimes we're the help-ees.

The helping others part is a cakewalk. We feel good when we reach out to people in need. When the tables are turned, though, our attitude may change. If we find our identity in helping others, we may struggle with the idea of others helping us.

Galatians 6:5 makes it clear that we should be as open to receiving help as we are to offering it. If that thought makes you uncomfortable, below are some suggestions that may help.

Swallow your pride.

The Bible teaches that pride has no place in a healthy person's life (see Proverbs 11:2, for example). Sometimes we try to disguise our pride as concern for others ("You should be helping someone who *really* needs it")—but we don't fool anyone. Pride isn't the product of self-confidence; it's the product of self-deception. If we allow our pride to get in the way of asking for help when we need it, we're dangerously deceived.

Admit your need.

No one makes it through this life unscathed. We all have times when a situation, illness, or problem gets the best of us. We all have times when we need a helping hand. When that happens to us, there's no shame in admitting it.

Give other people a chance to help you.

We know what it's like to make a difference in someone else's life. When we swallow our pride and admit our own needs, we give other people a chance to experience those things too.

Recognize that the tables may be turned next time.

Everyone experiences highs and lows. The people who are up today may be down tomorrow. If you give people an opportunity to help you when you need it, there's a pretty good chance they will return the favor someday. ■

Don't Let the Sun Go

One of the best-known and oft-quoted pieces of relationship advice is found in Ephesians 4:26. That's where the apostle Paul wrote, "Don't get so angry that you sin. Don't go to bed angry."

30

What's remarkable about the verse, though, is not just what it says but also what it doesn't say. The apostle Paul did not say, "Don't get angry" or "Anger is a sin." Instead, he warned us not to let our anger cause us to sin. Anger is a healthy emotion, every bit as valuable to our well-being as joy and grief. Anger is a natural response to upsetting circumstances.

Neither does the verse say, "Don't get angry with someone you love." That's unreasonable. When two people try to build a life together, conflict is inevitable. If they have problems resolving their conflicts, anger is practically a given. And that's okay. Anger is not the enemy of a committed relationship; indifference is. Healthy anger—the kind that is channeled and expressed properly—can produce positive results. At the very least, it signals a willingness to express your feelings to your loved one.

Ephesians 4:26 doesn't say, "Get rid of your anger immediately." That would be faulty advice. Like grief, anger needs to be processed. We need time to work through our feelings and then put words to them. Trying to resolve a conflict before we complete those steps will only lead to frustration and further anger.

What the apostle Paul suggested in Ephesians 4:26 is that we resolve our anger in a timely manner—ideally, within a day.

Down on Your Anger

Why?

One reason is that anger must not be allowed to fester. If it does, it will mutate into something uglier. Turned outward, it will become hatred; turned inward, depression. Clearing the air during your waking hours will prevent both scenarios.

A second reason to work through your anger before sleep overtakes you is that it lets you get on with your life sooner. Anger—and the grudges that result from it—will occupy your thoughts until you do something about it. The more quickly you deal with it, the less your productivity will suffer.

A third reason to deal with anger today instead of tomorrow is that tomorrow is promised to no one. Too many people regret their last angry words to a loved one. Don't allow yourself to become one of them. Don't go to bed angry. ■

Words of
WISDOM

EPHESIANS 4:25–32

We are part of the same body. Stop lying and start telling each other the truth. Don't get so angry that you sin. Don't go to bed angry and don't give the devil a chance.

If you are a thief, quit stealing. Be honest and work hard, so you will have something to give to people in need.

Stop all your dirty talk. Say the right thing at the right time and help others by what you say.

Don't make God's Spirit sad. The Spirit makes you sure that someday you will be free from your sins.

Stop being bitter and angry and mad at others. Don't yell at one another or curse each other or ever be rude. Instead, be kind and merciful, and forgive others, just as God forgave you because of Christ.

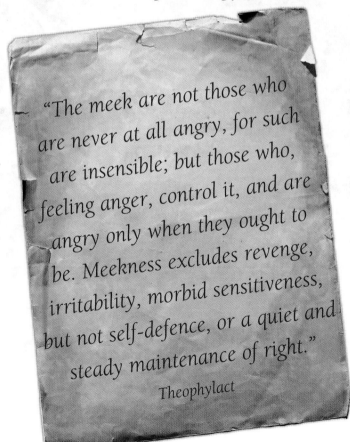

"The meek are not those who are never at all angry, for such are insensible; but those who, feeling anger, control it, and are angry only when they ought to be. Meekness excludes revenge, irritability, morbid sensitiveness, but not self-defence, or a quiet and steady maintenance of right."

Theophylact

31

Work As If God Were Your Boss

How would your work habits change if God were your boss? Not someone with a God complex, mind you—but God himself. What if he were in your workplace every day, observing you as you went about your business?

That's the scenario the apostle Paul raised as he offered the following advice to workers everywhere: "Do your work willingly, as though you were serving the Lord himself, and not just your earthly master" (Colossians 3:23).

If our work is part of our service to God, we need to look for instructions we can apply in the workplace. The Bible provides us with many examples.

"Jesus then said, 'So it is. Everyone who is now last will be first, and everyone who is first will be last.' " (Matthew 20:16)

This principle adds a wrinkle to the notion of getting ahead in our careers. At the very least, it makes us reconsider the importance of promotions.

"When you make a promise, say only 'Yes' or 'No.' Anything else comes from the devil." (Matthew 5:37)

This instruction gets to the heart of integrity in the workplace— whether between coworkers or between the company and its customers. It prohibits the double-talk and excuses that can sour the workplace atmosphere.

"God will judge everything we do, even what is done in secret, whether good or bad." (Ecclesiastes 12:14)

Knowing that God can see everything would certainly cut down on the time-killing diversions that keep people from doing their jobs. It would inspire us to manage our time better.

"Love others as much as you love yourself." (Mark 12:31)

This principle has special resonance for jobs that put us in contact with the public. "Loving others" is light years beyond "The customer is always right." To love others is to actively seek what's best for them.

Wisdom

T. W. MANSON

"In the Kingdom of God, service is not a stepping-stone to nobility: it is nobility, the only kind of nobility that is recognized."

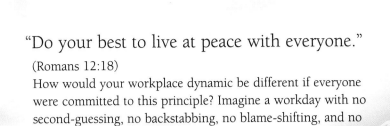

"Do your best to live at peace with everyone."

(Romans 12:18)

How would your workplace dynamic be different if everyone were committed to this principle? Imagine a workday with no second-guessing, no backstabbing, no blame-shifting, and no office politics.

"When you eat or drink or do anything else, always do it to honor God." (1 Corinthians 10:31)

Work certainly has a place on that list. To apply this principle is to preface every work-related decision with the question, What would best honor God? ■

32

Get Involved
in Church

How often do you make it to church? Do you consider it a priority? Do you treat it as a priority? The author of Hebrews made it clear that church is essential for our well-being.

"Some people have given up the habit of meeting for worship, but we must not do that. We should keep on encouraging each other, especially since you know that the day of the Lord's coming is getting closer" (Hebrews 10:25).

Church addresses three important needs in our lives that we may not even be aware of.

Church fulfills our need for worship.

When we understand who God is and what he's done, worship becomes a natural response. Worship is simply giving God his due. When we set aside time every week to praise him, thank him, sing about him, and listen to stories about his incredible work, we're showing him that we "get it"—that we understand (as much as we're able to) how incredible he is.

Some people prefer to worship God outside of church, in the solitude and beauty of nature. There's certainly benefit in that. However, in a church setting with like-minded believers, something special happens. Our worship multiplies and becomes greater than the sum of its parts.

Church fulfills our need for companionship.

It's a simple fact that we need regular interaction with other people who share our beliefs. Spending time with people who find joy in their faith, who base their lives on the Bible's teachings, and who face the same struggles and challenges we face is good for the soul.

As we interact with other believers, we sharpen one another's dull edges and rough patches. We become better and more useful followers of Christ.

Church fulfills our need for spiritual growth.

There are only two settings on the Christian life: growth and stagnation. If we're not actively growing, week by week, in our faith and in our knowledge of God and the Bible, we're going nowhere.

Reading the Bible on our own is a great start, but it's only a start. We need to hear what experts say about it—people who have studied and taught it for years. We need to understand the context of certain passages, the historical background of each story, the full implications of Jesus' teachings. We need to learn from people who know more than we do. ∎

He decided how many stars there would

PSALM 147:4

Look at the evening sky!
Who created the stars?
Who gave them each a name?
Who leads them like an army?
The Lᴏʀᴅ is so powerful
That none of the stars
are ever missing.

Isaiah 40:26

be in the sky and gave each one a name.

Treat Sex as

33

The idea of two people becoming one is as old as humankind. Genesis 2:21–23 describes God's creation of woman from man. Then Genesis 2:24 says, "That's why a man will leave his own father and mother. He marries a woman, and the two of them become like one person."

That coming together is sacred, as far as God is concerned. And he wants it to be sacred to us too. The writer of Hebrews made that abundantly clear: "Have respect for marriage. Always be faithful to your partner, because God will punish anyone who is immoral or unfaithful in marriage" (Hebrews 13:4).

With our wedding vows, we commit ourselves to the same zeal for marriage that God has. We commit to being vigilant in protecting, preserving, and celebrating our intimate relationship with our spouse.

You can find hundreds of books, programs, and seminars devoted to maintaining a healthy marriage. Though they all offer different spins on the topic, most agree on a few key strategies. ■

Words of WISDOM

COLOSSIANS 3:14

Love is more important than anything else. It is what ties everything completely together.

LOVE

1. strong liking or affection of something or someone 2. a passionate affection from one person to another 3. the object of such affection; a sweetheart

Sacred

KEEP AN OPEN LINE OF COMMUNICATION WITH YOUR SPOUSE.

Talk frequently about your relationship—what you love about it as well as what you'd like to change. The more comfortable you feel talking about your marriage, the better chance you have of making beneficial changes to it.

BE PROACTIVE IN DEALING WITH TEMPTING SITUATIONS.

Few people who violate their marriage vows set out with the specific intention of doing so. What usually happens is that they

- find themselves in situations they're not prepared for;
- allow a casual friendship to grow into something more;
- find something in someone else that they're not getting from their spouse.

The best way to avoid those situations is to nip them in the bud. Establish a set of personal rules for interacting with coworkers, neighbors, or acquaintances that you will not violate. Douse any smoldering embers for past flames.

DON'T WEAR A GROOVE IN YOUR RELATIONSHIP.

You wear a groove—or rut—in your relationship by doing what you've always done for no other reason than you've always done it. Once ruts are established, they can be difficult to escape. Over time, they can cause significant damage to your relationship.

Work hard to maintain a fresh and vibrant partnership with your spouse—one that's always growing, always moving in interesting directions. Anticipate your spouse's needs and find creative ways to fulfill them.

Listen Hard, Listen Well

The best gift you can give anyone is a listening ear. To listen to someone is to say, "You are important to me. I want to learn more about what you think and feel." That's why the apostle James recommended it so highly: "My dear friends, you should be quick to listen and slow to speak or to get angry" (James 1:19).

If you make a resolution to become a better listener, you'll quickly discover six important truths.

LISTENING CAN BE DIFFICULT.

Pausing long enough for a person to finish a sentence is not the same as listening. Hearing what someone says is not the same as listening. Listening is an art that requires a certain set of skills.

LISTENING REQUIRES CONCENTRATION.

When you listen to someone, you pick up not only their words but also the emotions behind them. You register not only what's being said but also what's not being said.

LISTENING ALMOST ALWAYS PRODUCES QUESTIONS.

When you're fully engaged in what someone is saying, you'll wonder about certain things. At the proper time, you'll ask leading questions to encourage the person to open up more, or you'll ask follow-up questions to help you understand better.

"THE FIRST DUTY OF LOVE IS TO LISTEN."

PAUL TILLICH

Earth and Sky,
  listen to what I say!
Israel, I will teach you.
My words will be like
gentle rain
  on tender young
  plants,
  or like dew on the grass.

Deuteronomy 32:1–2

LISTENING TAKES PRACTICE.

Once you get the skills down, though, people will seek you out. Everyone loves a good listener.

LISTENING IS A GREAT WAY TO LEARN.

Everyone you know—and everyone you meet—has knowledge and experience that you don't have. When you open your ears and mind to people, you get to share their knowledge and experience.

In order to be a great learner, you have to be a great listener. In order to be a great listener, you have to approach conversations with a humble attitude. You can't learn from someone until you acknowledge that the person has something to teach you.

LISTENING IS A GREAT WAY TO REDUCE CONFLICT.

Note how the apostle James contrasted being quick to listen with being slow to get angry. Usually at the heart of every conflict is someone who wants to be heard. If we oblige the person by listening, we may be able to head off conflict before it arises.

That's not to say we should always agree (or pretend to agree) with others during a conflict. But we should understand their point of view—and why they hold it—before we disagree with them. ■

Banish Snobbery

It's not hard to affirm that simple truth. Death strips us down to our essential being. Earthly riches are nothing special to God. Neither are social standing or power. Acts 10:34 teaches: "God treats all people alike." As far as God is concerned, everyone operates on a level playing field.

The apostle James urged us to follow God's example.

MY FRIENDS, IF YOU HAVE FAITH IN OUR GLORIOUS LORD JESUS CHRIST, YOU WON'T TREAT SOME PEOPLE BETTER THAN OTHERS. SUPPOSE A RICH PERSON WEARING FANCY CLOTHES AND A GOLD RING COMES TO ONE OF YOUR MEETINGS. AND SUPPOSE A POOR PERSON DRESSED IN WORN-OUT CLOTHES ALSO COMES. YOU MUST NOT GIVE THE BEST SEAT TO THE ONE IN FANCY CLOTHES AND TELL THE ONE WHO IS POOR TO STAND AT THE SIDE OR SIT ON THE FLOOR. THIS IS THE SAME AS SAYING THAT SOME PEOPLE ARE BETTER THAN OTHERS, AND YOU WOULD BE ACTING LIKE A CROOKED JUDGE.

MY DEAR FRIENDS, PAY ATTENTION. GOD HAS GIVEN A LOT OF FAITH TO THE POOR PEOPLE IN THIS WORLD. GOD HAS ALSO PROMISED THEM A SHARE IN HIS KINGDOM THAT HE WILL GIVE TO EVERYONE WHO LOVES HIM. YOU MISTREAT THE POOR. BUT ISN'T IT THE RICH WHO BOSS YOU AROUND AND DRAG YOU OFF TO COURT? AREN'T THEY THE ONES WHO MAKE FUN OF YOUR LORD?

James 2:1–7

James's point is valid. If there's any place where true equality should be found, it's the church—in the hearts of Jesus' followers. In order to make that a reality, though, we need to ask ourselves some difficult questions.

- Whom do I gravitate toward in social settings (like church)—and why?
- Whom do I avoid in those settings—and why?
- Do I derive satisfaction from being seen with the "right" people?
- Do I ever fall into the trap of interacting with people based on what they can do for me?
- Do I spend too much time around people I'm comfortable with?
- What conclusions might people draw about me based on my socializing choices? Would they be accurate?
- What do I need to do in order to align my socializing with the principles of James 2:1–7?
- What's the first step I will take this week? ■

We know what love is because Jesus gave his life for us. This is why we must give our lives for each other. If we have all we need and see one of our own people in need, we must have pity on that person, or else we cannot say we love God. Children, you show love for others by truly helping them, and not merely by talking about it.

1 John 3:16–18

36 Recognize the Power of Your Words

Forget Twelve-Week Body Shaping or Seven-Minute Abs. The apostle James said if you want a *real* workout, try controlling your tongue.

> By putting a bit into the mouth of a horse, we can turn the horse in different directions. It takes strong winds to move a large sailing ship, but the captain uses only a small rudder to make it go in any direction. Our tongues are small too, and yet they brag about big things.
>
> It takes only a spark to start a forest fire! The tongue is like a spark. It is an evil power that dirties the rest of the body and sets a person's entire life on fire with flames that come from hell itself. All kinds of animals, birds, reptiles, and sea creatures can be tamed and have been tamed. But our tongues get out of control. They are restless and evil, and always spreading deadly poison.
>
> My dear friends, with our tongues we speak both praises and curses. We praise our Lord and Father, and we curse people who were created to be like God, and this isn't right. (James 3:3–10)

If we're serious about making a difference in this world, we need to lead with our words. On the one hand, that involves reducing the damage we cause. We can do that by

- taking a walk to cool off instead of lashing out in an anger;

- refusing to talk negatively about people when they're not around;

- choosing not to tease people with comments that hit too close to home;

- keeping insults and backhanded compliments to ourselves;

- avoiding inappropriate jokes.

On the other hand, our words can be just as powerful in a positive way. We can make a difference in others' lives by

- making sincere apologies when they're necessary;

- sharing a good joke with people who will appreciate it;

- offering heartfelt compliments to friends, family members, acquaintances, and strangers alike;

- asking questions that demonstrate an interest in other people and encourage them to open up.

One way or another, your words will influence others. You have the power to determine what kind of impact it will be. ◼

GALATIANS 2:20

I HAVE DIED, BUT CHRIST LIVES IN ME. AND I NOW LIVE BY FAITH IN THE SON OF GOD, WHO LOVED ME AND GAVE HIS LIFE FOR ME.

37 Let Peace Start with You

PURE

If you want peace, work for justice. You've probably seen that slogan on a bumper sticker. Did you know it has biblical roots? Look at these words from the apostle James: "But the wisdom that comes from above leads us to be pure, friendly, gentle, sensible, kind, helpful, genuine, and sincere. When peacemakers plant seeds of peace, they will harvest justice" (James 3:17–18).

GENTLE James presented a different shade of meaning, perhaps, but the point remains: justice and peace are inevitably linked.

As followers of Jesus, we are called to be peacemakers, which means justice and peace should both be high on our priority list. But where do we go from there? What can we hope to achieve in a culture rife with injustice and conflict? How can we plant seeds of peace?

We can be slow to confront.

HELPFUL

Peace is rarely spread—or enjoyed—by people with thin skin. If you want to be a peacemaker, you need to make sure that your hide can withstand the arrows that will be fired your way. The fact is, people say dumb things—offensive things, self-glorifying things—all the time.

If our knee-jerk reaction is to confront people every time they offend us, we may be written off as humorless cranks. If, on the other hand, we choose our confrontational battles wisely, we will make more of an impact when we do speak up.

Toward that end, we must learn to let insults slide and minor infractions go unpunished. In other words, we shouldn't look for things to be offended about.

A Divine Work

"Now peacemaking is a divine work. For peace means reconciliation, and God is the author of peace and of reconciliation. . . . It is hardly surprising, therefore, that the particular blessing which attaches to peacemakers is that 'they shall be called sons of God.' For they are seeking to do what their Father has done, loving people with his love."

John R. W. Stott, *The Message of the Sermon on the Mount*

God blesses those people who make peace. They will be called his children! MATTHEW 5:9

SENSIBLE

KIND

GENUINE

We can be quick to say, "I'm sorry."

Genuine peace cannot exist where grudges are held and past offenses aren't forgiven. If you know you've wronged someone—or if you know someone who feels wronged by you—talk to the person. Find out exactly what the problem is.

If you see that you're at fault, even a little, admit it and ask for forgiveness. The only thing you have to lose is a little pride. The potential for gain, on the other hand, is tremendous.

We can stand against injustice—in any form.

Do you know someone who's being bullied or treated unfairly? Speak up. Stand alongside the person to show your support. Let your sense of fairness guide you. Work to bring peace to the person's life. ■

SINCERE

38 Keep Today in Perspective

What are you doing tomorrow? Actually, that's a trick question. Before you answer, you may want to read these words from the apostle James:

> You should know better than to say, "Today or tomorrow we will go to the city. We will do business there for a year and make a lot of money!" What do you know about tomorrow? How can you be so sure about your life? It is nothing more than mist that appears for only a little while before it disappears. You should say, "If the Lord lets us live, we will do these things." (James 4:13–15)

James wasn't trying to discourage people from planning ahead. In fact, the Bible encourages us repeatedly to prepare for the future. James was warning against

🐌 assuming tomorrow is a given;

🐌 having a false sense of security about tomorrow;

🐌 making our own plans for tomorrow without considering God's bigger plans for our future.

It's foolish to confidently predict what tomorrow will bring when we have absolutely no power over it. One accident, one chance encounter, one fateful decision, one freak occurrence, or one careless comment can change life as we know it and bring a tomorrow we've never anticipated. Who, other than God himself, can legitimately claim to know what will happen twenty-four hours from now? ■

"God delights to plan for His children. No human father ever experienced such joy in planning for his child as God experiences as He plans for you. He does not want you to miss any part of His beautiful purpose for you. His plans are filled with details of blessing, joy, and wonderful surprises."

Wesley L. Duewel

If the Lord lets us live, we will do these things.

With that in mind, how should a thoughtful, spiritual person approach tomorrow? Here are three ideas.

We should keep our personal accounts up to date.

Since tomorrow is guaranteed to no one, we can't know for sure that we'll have a chance beyond today to make apologies, offer congratulations, restore broken relationships, or tell loved ones what they mean to us. If you have an opportunity to do it today, jump on it. One day you may be glad you did.

We should stay humble.

Regardless of how detailed our five-, ten-, and twenty-year plans are, we're not holding the reins of our future. God is. We're at his mercy, so we would be wise to acknowledge that we aren't in control.

We should bathe our plans in prayer.

The wisest course of action is to run our projections past the Lord before we try to make them reality. When we pray, we ask God for guidance and trust that he will lead us in our decisions about tomorrow.

Get on Your Knees

Few things in the spiritual realm are more confounding than prayer. After all, if God already knows everything—and if he already has a plan in place for everyone—what can we hope to accomplish by talking to him?

Obviously there are complicated theological answers to those questions. But all we basically need to know is that the Bible puts a lot of stock in prayer. Just look at these words from the apostle James:

> If you are having trouble, you should pray. And if you are feeling good, you should sing praises. If you are sick, ask the church leaders to come and pray for you. Ask them to put olive oil on you in the name of the Lord. If you have faith when you pray for sick people, they will get well. The Lord will heal them, and if they have sinned, he will forgive them.

> If you have sinned, you should tell each other what you have done. Then you can pray for one another and be healed. The prayer of an innocent person is powerful, and it can help a lot. Elijah was just as human as we are, and for three and a half years his prayers kept the rain from falling. But when he did pray for rain, it fell from the skies and made the crops grow. (James 5:13–18)

If we acknowledge that prayer is important, our next step is to figure out how to pray; that is, what to say to God.

One of the most popular prayer models is called ACTS, an acronym for four key elements of prayer: adoration, confession, thanksgiving, and supplication. ■

Adoration

The best way to start any prayer is by telling God how awesome he is. The more specific you are in your praise and the more time you spend in adoration, the better your experience will be.

Confession

The things we do wrong get in the way of our relationship with God. To make things right, we need to confess them and ask for his forgiveness.

Thanksgiving

It's one thing to be thankful for the countless things God does for us; it's quite another to tell him, in detail, just how thankful we are.

Supplication

After we've told God that we recognize how incredible he is, asked his forgiveness, and thanked him, we can talk to him about our requests.

We are certain God will hear our prayers when we ask for what pleases him. And if we know God listens when we pray, we are sure our prayers have already been answered.

1 John 5:14–15

OUR FATHER

Jesus taught his disciples to pray.

When you pray, don't be like those show-offs who love to stand up and pray in the synagogues and on the street corners. They do this just to look good. I can assure you that they already have their reward.

When you pray, go into a room alone and close the door. Pray to your Father in private. He knows what is done in private and will reward you.

When you pray, don't talk on and on as people do who don't know God. They think God likes to hear long prayers. Don't be like them. Your Father knows what you need even before you ask.

Christ Taking Leave of the Apostles
Duccio (1260–1318)

You should pray like this:

Our Father in heaven,
help us to honor
your name.
Come and set up
your kingdom,
so that everyone on earth
will obey you,
as you are obeyed
in heaven.
Give us our food for today.
Forgive us for doing wrong,
as we forgive others.
Keep us from being tempted
and protect us from evil.

If you forgive others for the wrongs they do to you, your Father
in heaven will forgive you. But if you don't forgive others, your
Father will not forgive your sins.

Matthew 6:5–14

40 Spend Some Time in Nature

David, Israel's most famous king, was known as a man after God's own heart. The words he wrote in Psalm 19 reveal one of the reasons he earned this reputation.

"The heavens keep telling the wonders of God, and the skies declare what he has done. Each day informs the following day; each night announces to the next. They don't speak a word, and there is never the sound of a voice. Yet their message reaches all the earth, and it travels around the world" (Psalm 19:1–4).

David recognized that the character and nature of the Creator can be seen in his creation. If you want to get to know God better—and perhaps, like David, become a person after God's heart—spend time in nature.

Once upon a time, that didn't take much effort. People's work, play, and relaxation all took place outside. Nature was a constant companion. For some people today, that's still the case. But many of us have precious little contact with the natural world. Urbanization, technological advances, and the demand for comfort and convenience have dramatically reduced the number of hours we spend outside.

Why not reverse that trend? For the sake of your holistic well-being, make a purposeful decision to start enjoying the natural world. While you're out there, why not also get to know the One who made it? If you'd like to give it a try, consider these ideas:

DON'T JUST OBSERVE NATURE; STUDY IT.

Brush up on your biology, astronomy, geology, and botany. Reacquaint yourself with the natural processes you learned in school. Seek out connections in nature that you never noticed before.

KEEP A JOURNAL OF YOUR OBSERVATIONS.

Fill it with your thoughts about God and his creative works, questions that occur to you, or famous quotations that come to mind. You could even try your hand at the type of poetry David used to worship his God in Psalm 19.

Words of WISDOM

PSALM 104:5
You built foundations for the earth, and it will never be shaken.

TALK TO OTHERS ABOUT YOUR EXPERIENCES.

Encourage your friends and family to spend time in nature too. If you have kids, nurture their appreciation for God's creation. Share your observations, conclusions, and questions with each other.

TALK TO GOD ABOUT THE THINGS YOU SEE.

When you're awestruck by a sunset, tell God. Express your reaction through prayer. When you learn something new about the intricacies of the human body, share your amazement and gratitude. When you feel overwhelmed by the immensity of the universe, confess your feelings of insignificance. ■

41 Refuse to Rest on Your Laurels

Anyone who has studied the Greek tragedies understands the concept of *hubris*. In ancient Greek dramas, hubris was often the fatal flaw that led to the hero's downfall. After all, it's one thing to take satisfaction in a job well done; but it's quite another to view the world and make decisions with an overinflated human ego.

The Bible conveys a similar message. Proverbs 1:32, for example, is enough to wipe a smug expression off any face: "Sin and self-satisfaction bring destruction and death to stupid fools."

If that seems unnecessarily harsh, consider this: self-satisfaction causes us to claim credit that, according to the Bible, belongs to God.

Ironically, self-satisfaction also prevents us from finding out what we're really capable of. If we're content with what we've already done, we have no reason to strive for more. As a result, we never test our limitations. We never discover the extent of our abilities.

Rather than rest on our laurels, we should treat every milestone as a new starting line—another chance to prove ourselves using our God-given abilities. Leave yesterday's accomplishments to yesterday. Tomorrow's possibilities are endless. ∎

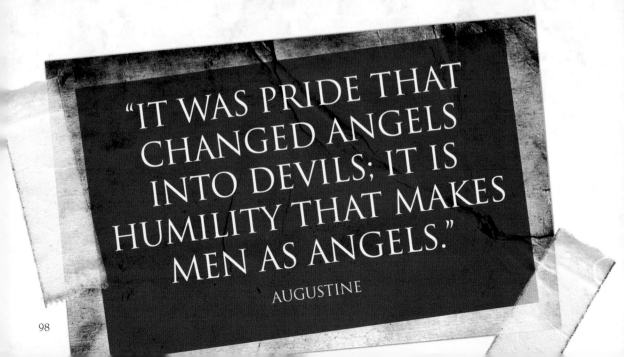

"IT WAS PRIDE THAT CHANGED ANGELS INTO DEVILS; IT IS HUMILITY THAT MAKES MEN AS ANGELS."

AUGUSTINE

42

Learn Something New Every Day

Solomon received unprecedented wisdom from God. He may have been the wisest person who ever lived.

Yet that was not enough for him. Even at the pinnacle of his wisdom, he hungered to learn more. Consider his words in Proverbs 9:9: "If you have good sense, instruction will help you to have even better sense. And if you live right, education will help you to know even more."

As far as Solomon was concerned, the word *enough* did not apply to learning. "To know even more" could well have been his motto. What held true for him is true for us as well: every day brings new opportunities to learn, explore, and expand our understanding.

Treasure troves of knowledge—not just facts and figures, but wisdom that helps you to live well—can be found almost anywhere. Cultivate a healthy sense of curiosity, and pursue knowledge wherever you can find it—not just in books or on websites, but also from the people you talk to and the natural world around you. ■

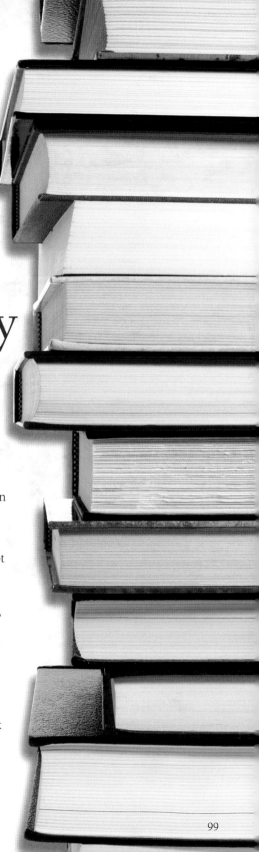

43 Develop Humility

From an early age, we are sold on the importance of confidence. We're told to remain confident in the face of opposition, carry ourselves with an air of confidence, and answer interview questions confidently.

After all, confidence is an attractive quality in a person. Confidence can put others at ease. It's a hallmark of great leaders.

Yet left unchecked, confidence can quickly morph into something more insidious: egotism. Egotism is an inflated sense of self-importance, which often leads to boasting. The writer of this biblical proverb had his sights set on egotism when he shared the following advice: "Don't ever think that you are wise enough, but respect the LORD and stay away from evil. This will make you healthy, and you will feel strong" (Proverbs 3:7–8).

The antidote to egotism is humility. Notice how the writer of this proverb contrasts "think[ing] that you are wise enough"—that is, having an overly high view of yourself—with respecting God. Recognizing a higher power offers surprising benefits: it provides perspective about our place in the greater scheme. Standing in a relationship with God is both ennobling and humbling.

To be humble is to recognize where your strengths come from. The truth is, there are very few things a person can claim credit for. Are you smart? You can thank God for allowing your brain to retain and process knowledge. Are you good-looking? You can thank God for your genetic code. Are you skilled in a particular sport or two? You can thank God for good hand-eye coordination.

Your role is to make the most of what God has given you. While you can (and should) take pride in your efforts, be sure the lion's share of credit is not misplaced.

To be humble is to give credit to others who contributed to your success. No one succeeds on their own, whether in school, a career, a family, or sports. Fellow students, coworkers, family members, and teammates all play crucial roles. To ignore this truth is to rob others of their due credit.

To be humble is also to be comfortable outside of the spotlight. Rather than pursue fame and call attention to yourself, work to become a person of quiet confidence, one who is quick to put God-given abilities to use—and even quicker to acknowledge the contributions of others. ∎

"DO YOU WISH TO RISE? BEGIN BY DESCENDING. YOU PLAN A TOWER THAT WILL PIERCE THE CLOUDS? LAY FIRST THE FOUNDATION OF HUMILITY."

AUGUSTINE

THE GRACE OF
Humilty

2 CHRONICLES 7:14

If my own people will humbly pray and turn back to me and stop sinning, then I will answer them from heaven. I will forgive them and make their land fertile once again.

1 PETER 5:5

All of you young people should obey your elders. In fact, everyone should be humble toward everyone else. The Scriptures say, "God opposes proud people, but he helps everyone who is humble."

PHILIPPIANS 2:3-11

Don't be jealous or proud, but be humble and consider others more important than yourselves. Care about them as much as you care about yourselves and think the same way that Christ Jesus thought: Christ was truly God. But he did not try to remain equal with God. Instead he gave up everything and became a slave, when he became like one of us. Christ was humble. He obeyed God and even died on a cross. Then God gave Christ the highest place and honored his name above all others. So at the name of Jesus everyone will bow down, those in heaven, on earth, and under the earth. And to the glory of God the Father everyone will openly agree, "Jesus Christ is Lord!"

44 Use Your Position to Do Good

A good helper is welcome practically anywhere, anytime. When a good helper shows up, people breathe a sigh of relief and gratitude. Situations improve immediately.

Solomon, the author of Proverbs 3, recognized the difference a good helper could make. That's why he offered the following advice: "Do all you can for everyone who deserves your help. Don't tell your neighbor to come back tomorrow, if you can help today" (Proverbs 3:27–28).

Being a good helper involves more than just a willing spirit, of course. We've all heard of (or experienced) situations where well-intentioned people made problems worse with their "help." To be a good helper, you must possess the following traits:

- an awareness of people's needs

- the right attitude toward the problem at hand

- a clear-eyed view of your own skills, abilities, and limitations

- a willingness to sacrifice your time and energy for someone else's sake

Some people are quick to ask for help. Others are uncomfortable with admitting their needs—whether because of pride, embarrassment, or fear of becoming an imposition. That's where listening is key. If you learn to read between the lines when people talk, you'll be able to pick up on some of their unspoken needs.

Some people have ongoing needs, based on their situation. For example, do you know a single parent who could use occasional childcare? Or perhaps an elderly couple who need their sidewalk shoveled during winter? Do you know of a disabled person who could use periodic transportation? Once you open your eyes to the needs around you, you'll find no shortage of them.

When you offer help, be sure to do so with humility. Avoid striking a hero's pose. You have skills that might be of use to someone else, that's all. In other circumstances, you might very well be the person who needs help.

Also, don't claim to be an expert if you aren't one. Don't oversell your abilities. The last thing you want to do is get in over your head when you're helping someone else. Where skills are concerned, stay within your comfort zone.

Finally, there's the matter of realistic sacrifice. How much time can you afford to give to others? If you can spare five hours a week, find someone who needs five hours of assistance. Don't commit to something bigger than your ability to help. ■

WISDOM

If we have all we need and see one of our own people in need, we must have pity on that person, or else we cannot say we love God.
1 JOHN 3:17

45 Choose Your Associates Carefully

Can you spot a bad person on the street? Can you look at someone and tell whether they have good intentions or not? Solomon, the author of Proverbs 4, understood that the ability to distinguish between good and bad people is crucial to spiritual and physical health.

"Don't follow the bad example of cruel and evil people. Turn aside and keep going. Stay away from them" (Proverbs 4:14–15).

The problem is that "cruel and evil" people are not always easily identified. It's not like they wear villainous costumes in real life. Some hide their cruelty behind masks of humor. They say hurtful things and claim they're only kidding. Still others practice their cruelty in secret, behind the scenes. They use gossip and lies to ruin reputations and manipulate others.

Before you allow someone else to influence you, try to ascertain a few things about their character. It's not always easy, but here are a few steps.

Take a look at the people who influence them.
What are those people known for? Is it helping others or hurting them? Generally speaking, people of good character surround themselves with good influences.

Look at their priorities.
Instead of only listening to what they say is important to them, pay close attention to what they spend most of their time doing. People demonstrate their real priorities through their actions.

DON'T FOOL YOURSELVES. BAD FRIENDS WILL DESTROY YOU.
1 CORINTHIANS 15:33

Look at the fruit of their labor.
Do they leave wounded, betrayed people in their wake? Do they have a good reputation among those whose opinions you respect? Has anyone tried to warn you about associating with them?

If you come to the conclusion that someone is evil, cruel, or just potentially a bad influence, your best bet is to make a clean break—or as clean as you can. Minimize that person's influence on your life by spending as little time with them as possible. Don't be fooled by empty promises or protestations of innocence. If you believe someone is going to impact your life negatively, you have a responsibility to do something about it.

Once you've severed ties and protected yourself from bad influence, pray for that person. Ask God to work in his or her life and help turn evil intentions into good. God is very good at that. ■

THE WISDOM OF A
Father

My child, listen closely to my teachings and learn common sense.
My advice is useful, so don't turn away.
When I was still very young and my mother's favorite child, my father said to me:
"If you follow my teachings and keep them in mind, you will live.
Be wise and learn good sense; remember my teachings and do what I say.

If you love Wisdom and don't reject her, she will watch over you.
The best thing about Wisdom is Wisdom herself; good sense is more important than anything else.
If you value Wisdom and hold tightly to her, great honors will be yours.
It will be like wearing a glorious crown of beautiful flowers.

My child, if you listen and obey my teachings, you will live a long time.
I have shown you the way that makes sense; I have guided you along the right path.
Your road won't be blocked, and you won't stumble when you run.
Hold firmly to my teaching and never let go. It will mean life for you.
Don't follow the bad example of cruel and evil people.
Turn aside and keep going. Stay away from them.
They can't sleep or rest until they do wrong or harm some innocent victim.
Their food and drink are cruelty and wickedness.

The lifestyle of good people is like sunlight at dawn that keeps getting brighter until broad daylight.
The lifestyle of the wicked is like total darkness, and they will never know what makes them stumble.

My child, listen carefully to everything I say. Don't forget a single word, but think about it all.
Knowing these teachings will mean true life and good health for you.
Carefully guard your thoughts because they are the source of true life.
Never tell lies or be deceitful in what you say.
Keep looking straight ahead, without turning aside.
Know where you are headed, and you will stay on solid ground.
Don't make a mistake by turning to the right or the left.

IF YOU SLEEP
ALL THE TIME,
YOU WILL STARVE;

IF YOU GET UP AND WORK, YOU WILL HAVE ENOUGH FOOD.

PROVERBS 20:13

46
Be Prepared

It's not often that we look to the insect world for guidance. Yet that's exactly what Proverbs 6:6–8 encourages us to do: "You lazy people can learn by watching an anthill. Ants don't have leaders, but they store up food during harvest season."

The author of this proverb admired the ant's self-discipline—the instinct that compelled the tiny insect to gather provisions while they were still available and save them for when they weren't. Such a wise example carries four important lessons for us.

Harvests, literal or figurative, should not be taken for granted.

The opportunity to gather provisions—to earn money or build a surplus—is not always available. That's why it's important to make the most of every opportunity while we can. The ant doesn't sit out a harvest cycle to figure out what it wants to do with its life. It gathers while the gathering is good.

If you have a chance to build a surplus—to do work that rewards you with pay or benefits—do it while you can, for as long as you can.

Fortunes can turn in an instant.

If the "dot-com bubble" collapse of 2000–2001 or the "real estate bubble" collapse of 2007 taught us anything, it's that when things seem too good to be true, financially speaking, they probably are.

Learn from history. Don't fall into the trap of believing you're immune from a reversal of fortune. Remember, what seems like a long-term upward market trend may turn out to be a blip. And a promotion today does not negate the possibility of a demotion tomorrow. Make sure you're prepared for such possibilities.

Productivity should be a constant.

The author of Ecclesiastes tells us there is a season for everything, including planting and reaping (Ecclesiastes 3:2). That suggests a continuous cycle. If you do not reap when it's time to reap, you could be out of step with the natural rhythms of life.

Relying on others to do the work for you is counterproductive.

Working to provide for our needs, along with the needs of our families, can give us a sense of pride, accomplishment, and purpose. The satisfaction that comes from storing up provisions—that is, from reaping the benefits of an honest day's work—cannot be overstated. Every person who is physically capable should experience it. ■

47 Be Stronger Than Your Temptations

Even if you live by a moral code, you will face challenges to your convictions. Temptation found Adam and Eve in the Garden of Eden. It found Jesus in the wilderness. And it will find you—likely when you're at your most vulnerable point.

You might as well heed this advice from Proverbs and prepare yourself to face temptation: "Obey the teaching of your parents—always keep it in mind and never forget it. Their teaching will guide you when you walk, protect you when you sleep, and talk to you when you are awake. The Law of the Lord is a lamp, and its teachings shine brightly. Correction and self-control will lead you through life" (Proverbs 6:20–23).

As the author of Proverbs 6 recommended, meditating on the principles that form the core of who you are and who you should be is a great first step in resisting temptation. For the ancient Israelites, those core guiding principles were found in Scripture. A great many people still find the practice of reflection to be a helpful tool.

Here are a few other time-tested strategies you may want to consider.

Recognize where you're vulnerable.

Do you have a hard time saying no to your friends? Do you find it easier to lie than to tell uncomfortable truths? Are you susceptible to sexual enticements? If you know where your weaknesses are, you can plan accordingly. The key is being honest with yourself about your vulnerabilities.

Practice your escape routes.

Periodically ask yourself "What if" questions. What if an attractive married coworker started showing an interest in you? What if a friend asked you to do something that violated your conscience? You won't be able to predict every temptation that will come your way, but you can develop some strategies that apply to more than one scenario.

Enlist the assistance of others.

Find a trustworthy friend or a group with whom you can share your struggles. Knowing that another person is invested in your success or that you'll have to answer to someone for what you've done can mean the difference between a temptation successfully resisted and one that's not.

Celebrate your victories—but not too much.

When you manage to resist a tempting situation, give thanks to God for his assistance—and then give yourself a little pat on the back too. Make a mental note of the strategies that worked for you so that you can use them again.

Learn from your failures.

When you lose a battle to temptation, don't concede the war. Come back stronger next time. Resolve not to make the same mistake twice. ■

48

Be Unstoppable

What does it take to stop you? What is the kryptonite to your Superman? What, besides death, could halt your forward momentum in this world? Knowing the answer to this question could mean the difference between a life well-lived and one spent wondering what might have been.

The apostle Paul understood the importance of endurance. You can almost hear the pleading encouragement in his words to the Galatian church: "Don't get tired of helping others. You will be rewarded when the time is right, if you don't give up" (Galatians 6:9).

In order to live well, you need to be unstoppable in helping others. You will get tired; you might even want to quit at times and only focus on your own needs. Be aware of your vulnerabilities, and figure out how to keep your involvement fresh and interesting. A little preventive maintenance now will go a long way toward keeping you viable later.

Caring for the needs of others can be demanding, but it can also be immensely rewarding—both now and for eternity. ■

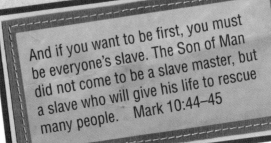

And if you want to be first, you must be everyone's slave. The Son of Man did not come to be a slave master, but a slave who will give his life to rescue many people. Mark 10:44–45

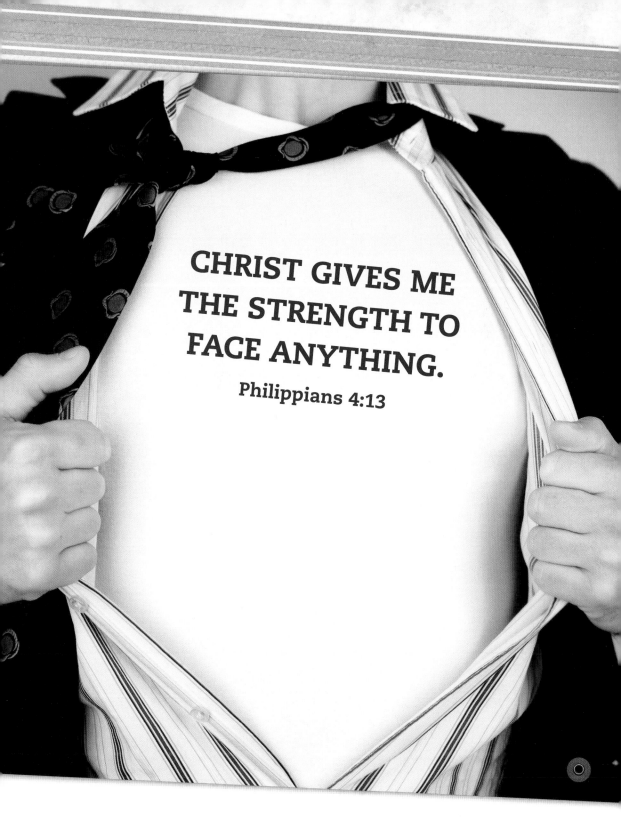

CHRIST GIVES ME THE STRENGTH TO FACE ANYTHING.

Philippians 4:13

Collect Knowledge

49

THE SOURCE OF WISDOM AND KNOWLEDGE

All wisdom comes from the LORD, and so do common sense and understanding. . . .

With wisdom you will learn what is right and honest and fair.

Wisdom will control your mind, and you will be pleased with knowledge. Sound judgment and good sense will watch over you.

Proverbs 2:6, 9–11

"Learn all you can, and can all you learn." That's how one person summarized Proverbs 10:14. Here's how the author of this proverb put it: "If you have good sense, you will learn all you can, but foolish talk will soon destroy you."

Lifelong learning is a key component of the pursuit of wisdom. The sayings in the book of Proverbs were compiled to champion the cause of wisdom and to inspire people everywhere to pursue it. Knowledge, as it turns out, is the fuel that powers wisdom.

Through the learning process, we gather raw information. Wisdom is the process of connecting bits of knowledge and applying them to our lives. The more we learn, the more opportunities we have to put our wisdom to use.

While there are countless ways in which knowledge affects our lives, there are a few key reasons why we should make collecting knowledge a priority.

Collecting knowledge is an excellent way to honor our Creator.

As the saying goes, "All truth is God's truth." It follows, then, that the more curious we are about ourselves, one another, and the world around us, the more we will appreciate the One ultimately responsible for it all. (It's also a great way to exercise the brains God gave us.)

Collecting knowledge gives us common ground with other people.

The more we learn, the more we can share knowledge with others—and benefit from their knowledge. If we're able to speak intelligently and ask thoughtful questions about a number of topics, we can lay the groundwork for meaningful connections with others.

Collecting knowledge can help us maintain a humble outlook on the world.

If we see ourselves as lifelong students, we're less likely to become full of ourselves. In addition, the more knowledge we acquire, the more we realize how little we really know. (Bragging or showing off knowledge would almost certainly fall under the "foolish talk" category of Proverbs 10:14.)

Keep in mind that knowledge doesn't just come from books or websites. Every experience in life, whether good or bad, can be a learning experience if you approach it the right way. Every conversation can teach you something, if you let it.

The secret is to maintain a highly curious outlook. Look for the nuggets of knowledge embedded all around you. If you approach everyday life with a hunger for learning, you will be satisfied. ■

50 Keep Good Company

Everyday life would be much easier to navigate if people's character and motives were immediately obvious. Imagine the disappointment, heartache, and trouble we could avoid if we could instantly identify liars, users, backstabbers, con artists, and people with ulterior motives.

We cannot, of course. And that leaves good-hearted, trusting people vulnerable to those who are less good-hearted and more conniving.

Solomon understood that truth better than most. As king of Israel, he had to deal with double-dealing associates, backstabbing underlings, and power-hungry rivals every day. Yet he survived—and thrived. And he offered the secret to his success in Proverbs 2:12–15: "Wisdom will protect you from evil schemes and from those liars who turned from doing good to live in the darkness. Most of all they enjoy being mean and deceitful. They are dishonest themselves, and so are all their deeds."

Wisdom evens the playing field. If we take a thoughtful, deliberate, well-reasoned approach to our interpersonal relationships, we can weed out the people who have no business in our lives.

Solomon understood two very important points regarding relationships:

🪶 You are judged by the company you keep.

🪶 You are influenced by the company you keep.

So if you fail to choose your friends and associates wisely, you will feel the impact—from without and within.

How do you apply wisdom to your interpersonal relationships? Carefully and objectively evaluate people before you allow them into your orbit. Don't give the benefit of the doubt to people who haven't earned it, and don't operate under the assumption that everyone is harmless until proven otherwise.

Before you allow people into your everyday life, you need to know and understand them pretty well. Toward that end, you should ask yourself some tough questions:

🪶 Why is this person interested in me? Do I have something she wants? Is she using me to get ahead?

🪶 Does this person seem to have my best interests at heart? Has he demonstrated an interest in my opinions and well-being?

🪶 Does this person have a proven track record? What do other people say about her? What do my friends and family members think of her?

The kind of people you surround yourself with says a lot about you. Choose them wisely. ■

You are judged by the company you keep.

The influence of others will affect your direction in life.

Give your friends and family a say in who influences you.

PHILIPPIANS 4:6-7

DON'T WORRY ABOUT ANYTHING, BUT PRAY ABOUT EVERYTHING. WITH THANKFUL HEARTS OFFER UP YOUR PRAYERS AND REQUESTS TO GOD. THEN, BECAUSE YOU BELONG TO CHRIST JESUS, GOD WILL BLESS YOU WITH PEACE THAT NO ONE CAN COMPLETELY UNDERSTAND. AND THIS PEACE WILL CONTROL THE WAY YOU THINK AND FEEL.

51 Stop Being Rude

In our culture, which encourages anonymous postings on social media sites and instant commentary on every news story (big and small), rudeness has become a way of life. Experts fear that even the most basic social graces are being lost as a result.

Two thousand years ago, the apostle Paul established a social standard that should still apply for people today as we interact with the world around us: "Love is . . . never . . . rude" (1 Corinthians 13:4–5).

That's a tall order, to be sure. At the very least, it forces us to examine our ability to interact with others in a pleasing, productive, and ultimately loving way. Toward that end, below are some questions to ask yourself about your social skills.

HELLO
my name is

Me Myself I

Am I an alert socializer?

Can I read body language? Can I pick up on a person's physical and verbal cues? Can I tell when it's time to engage and when it's time to back off? Can I tell when to end an encounter?

Am I an appropriate socializer?

Do I respect people's personal space? Do I avoid coarse language? Do I stay away from inappropriate remarks? Do people of both genders feel comfortable around me? Do I tend to push the limits when it comes to good taste?

Am I an engaging conversationalist?

Am I able to steer conversations from shallow topics to deeper ones? Do my stories hold people's interest? Am I able to involve everyone in the group in the conversation?

Do I dominate conversation?

Do people seem to go out of their way to avoid talking to me? Do I have a good grasp of the give-and-take of conversation? Do I really listen to what other people say, or do I just wait for them to finish so that I can talk again?

Do I show appropriate curiosity about other people's lives?

Do I remember key details about them? Do I enjoy learning new things from them? Do I ask thoughtful questions? Do I draw people into conversations?

Can I be trusted with personal information?

Am I susceptible to gossip? Have I put a strain on friendships in the past by sharing too much information about a person with someone else?

Avoiding rudeness involves more than just being polite. It involves making the people around us feel comfortable, respected, and cared for. ∎

Guard Your Thoughts

52

I don't like you right now...

SEXUAL TEMPTATION
ANGER
DOUBT
...ERNESS
...OYALTY

Wisdom

PHILIPPIANS 4:8

Finally, my friends, keep your minds on whatever is true, pure, right, holy, friendly, and proper. Don't ever stop thinking about what is truly worthwhile and worthy of praise.

In the American justice system, first-degree murder is treated as a more serious crime than other forms of homicide—and the sentences reflect that fact. Convictions for first-degree murder result in much longer prison terms than convictions for other life-taking offenses.

The difference is intent. Generally speaking, first-degree murder involves premeditation—some sort of planning. The fact that the crime is contemplated in advance makes it more heinous in the eyes of the judicial system. The reasoning is that someone who thinks about a crime beforehand has the wherewithal to prevent it from happening.

Unfortunately, the number of first-degree murder convictions in the United States suggests otherwise. Apparently thoughts can be powerful persuaders.

King Solomon was spreading that message thousands of years before the American justice system was established. He understood the power of the mind perhaps better than anyone. That's why he issued this heartfelt warning: "Carefully guard your thoughts because they are the source of true life" (Proverbs 4:23).

Be careful about what motivates you, he warned. Guard yourself against bad influences. If they're not properly checked, thoughts can take on a life of their own. Certainly first-degree murder is a rare extreme. But unguarded thoughts can wreak havoc in other ways too.

Here are some tips for guarding your thoughts.

DON'T DWELL ON SEXUAL TEMPTATION.

For many people, sexual thoughts are especially troublesome. A casual double entendre or a fleeting image in a TV commercial can be enough to start the mind drifting toward inappropriate thoughts. Unchecked, those thoughts can snowball into inappropriate actions.

To check those thoughts, we need to recognize them as inappropriate and call a mental time-out before thinking turns to fantasizing. A quick prayer and a walk to clear your head can often facilitate that process.

DON'T SAVOR ANGER.

Like sexual temptation, unchecked anger can blossom into something much more troubling. That's why it must be destroyed at the root level. When people upset you, acknowledge it—to yourself and to them. Give them a chance to make it right. If they do, be quick to offer forgiveness. If they don't, turn the matter over to God and move on.

DON'T HARBOR SILENT DOUBTS.

If you have a question for God, ask it. Pray about it. Seek answers in Scripture. Talk to spiritual leaders. Don't harbor thoughts that will damage your relationship with him simply because you don't understand his ways. ■

Thank you

53 Give Generously

"Generosity will be rewarded: Give a cup of water, and you will receive a cup of water in return" (Proverbs 11:25).

What's interesting about this verse is that Solomon, the writer, didn't say where the second cup of water will come from. He simply pointed out that what goes around comes around.

The simple act of giving to other people should be its own reward. Yet God sweetens the pot for us.

One good deed leads to another, and another—like a toppling domino chain—until eventually it comes back to you. Like a pebble dropped into a pond, one act of generosity can create a ripple effect that continues far beyond your field of vision.

Payback should never be our motivation in giving generously to other people. Still, it is nice to know that God is looking out for us, making sure that no good deed goes unrewarded. ■

Let That Insult Slide

54

You're going about your business when someone tosses an insult your way, and not in a joking manner, either. How do you respond? Do you give back just as good as you got? Or do you ignore the person and the insult?

Words of
WISDOM

ROMANS 14:10–12

Why do you criticize other followers of the Lord? Why do you look down on them? The day is coming when God will judge all of us. In the Scriptures God says,

"I swear by my very life that everyone will kneel down and praise my name!"

And so, each of us must give an account to God for what we do.

Not surprisingly, the Bible advocates the more challenging option. "Losing your temper is foolish; ignoring an insult is smart" (Proverbs 12:16).

Responding well to an insult takes self-control. It is not easy, but it can be done. Here's how.

Take a moment to mull it over.

When someone insults you, pause for a couple of beats before you respond. If you know the person, consider the source. Is the insult out of character for him? Have other people had problems with him?

Consider the person's circumstances. Might he be having a bad day? Might he be taking out his frustrations on you? Might he be feeling insecure about something?

Consider the person's intent. Is he trying to hurt your feelings? Is he trying to make you look bad? Is he trying to point out something you need to be aware of?

Consider your own role in the matter. Do you have a history with the person? Have you done anything to provoke anger or frustration? Does the person have a reason to want to hurt your feelings?

Say a quick prayer.

Send up a quick prayer to God. Ask him to give you the wisdom and understanding you need to respond to the insult in a way that pleases him. Ask him for the patience to deal with the person in a calm manner. Ask him for guidance in deciding whether to say anything or not. And ask him for the right words to say if you decide to respond.

Choose to take the high road.

If you do choose to respond to the person who insults you, get his side of the story. Find out why he insulted you. Let him know how you feel about it. Whatever you do, though, don't get drawn into a conflict. And don't stoop to repaying insult for insult.

Remember Jesus' words in Matthew 5:39: "I tell you not to try to get even with a person who has done something to you. When someone slaps your right cheek, turn and let that person slap your other cheek." ■

55 Surround Yourself with Wise People

If you ever get the sense you're not as wise as you'd like to be, look around at your friends. They may be partially to blame. At least, that's what Solomon, the author of Proverbs 13, believed.

"Wise friends make you wise, but you hurt yourself by going around with fools" (Proverbs 13:20).

On a scale of one to ten—with ten being King Solomon—how would you rate your closest friends based on their wisdom? More importantly, what effect is their collective wisdom (or lack of it) having on you?

Take a proactive approach to your emotional and spiritual growth. Choose the people who will—and won't—be allowed to influence you.

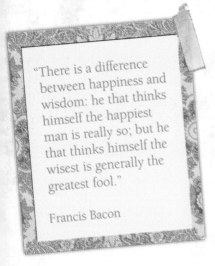

"There is a difference between happiness and wisdom: he that thinks himself the happiest man is really so; but he that thinks himself the wisest is generally the greatest fool."

Francis Bacon

Scale back your relationships with fools.

If it seems harsh to identify a friend as a fool, keep in mind that the Bible pulls no punches. Anyone who stands in the way of our spiritual growth is a fool.

You can identify fools by the choices they make, the priorities they hold, and the things they encourage you to do. If certain friends have shown a pattern of suffering negative consequences for their actions, if they put way too much emphasis on unimportant things, or if they bring out the worst in you, there's a good chance they fit the biblical definition of a fool.

That's not to say you should abandon those friends completely. You just need to remove them from a position of influence in your life. Don't allow them to tempt you with foolishness.

Spend more time with people who fit the criteria of being wise.

Since there is no standardized test for wisdom, you must use your best judgment. Look for people who are respected by their peers, people who are hard workers, people who have a reputation for honesty, and people whose Christian beliefs are evident in the way they live. None of those things necessarily guarantees that the person is wise, but each is a pretty good indicator.

Surround yourself with a variety of wise people who will stretch you and encourage you to grow. ∎

PROVERBS 4:5–7

BE WISE AND LEARN GOOD SENSE; REMEMBER MY TEACHINGS AND DO WHAT I SAY. IF YOU LOVE WISDOM AND DON'T REJECT HER, SHE WILL WATCH OVER YOU. THE BEST THING ABOUT WISDOM IS WISDOM HERSELF; GOOD SENSE IS MORE IMPORTANT THAN ANYTHING ELSE.

BE KIND TO EACH OTHER

Show Kindness

Sometimes small matters are the ones that have the biggest impact. Consider these words from Proverbs 15:1: "A kind answer soothes angry feelings, but harsh words stir them up."

At first glance, this seems like a routine directive to be nice to others. Yet it has the potential to change your outlook, your reputation, and even your health.

Harsh words are the product of anger and stress. Kind words, on the other hand, result from a calm, balanced, stress-free mind-set.

Kind words project an aura of confidence, maturity, and concern for others—all of which are extremely attractive qualities. Making a habit of responding to others with kind words will cause them to reevaluate their opinion of you. That's how reputations are built—and rehabilitated.

If you make kindness your default mode when dealing with others, you may also start to view people in a different way. Rather than seeing them as competitors who must be defeated in a conflict, you can see them as potential allies who bring valuable perspectives to the table or, at the very least, individuals who deserve to be heard. ■

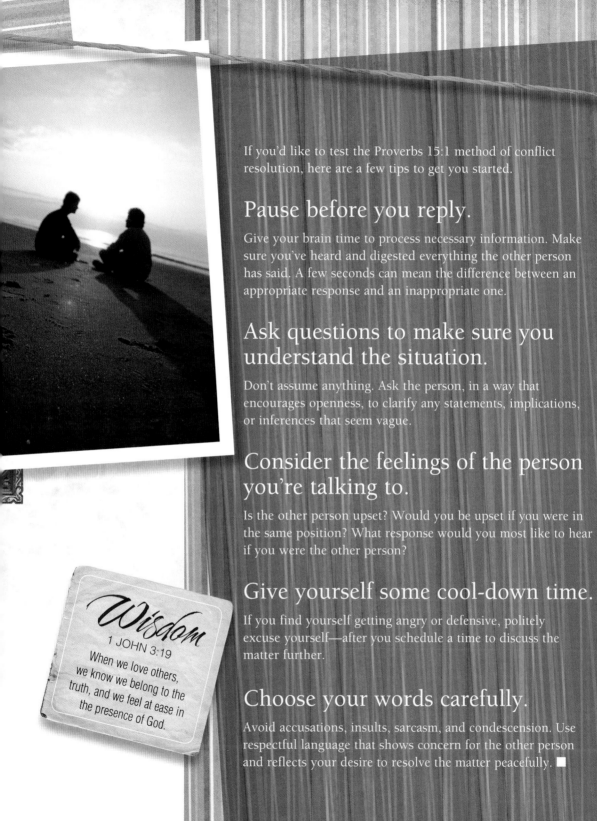

If you'd like to test the Proverbs 15:1 method of conflict resolution, here are a few tips to get you started.

Pause before you reply.

Give your brain time to process necessary information. Make sure you've heard and digested everything the other person has said. A few seconds can mean the difference between an appropriate response and an inappropriate one.

Ask questions to make sure you understand the situation.

Don't assume anything. Ask the person, in a way that encourages openness, to clarify any statements, implications, or inferences that seem vague.

Consider the feelings of the person you're talking to.

Is the other person upset? Would you be upset if you were in the same position? What response would you most like to hear if you were the other person?

Give yourself some cool-down time.

If you find yourself getting angry or defensive, politely excuse yourself—after you schedule a time to discuss the matter further.

Choose your words carefully.

Avoid accusations, insults, sarcasm, and condescension. Use respectful language that shows concern for the other person and reflects your desire to resolve the matter peacefully. ∎

Wisdom

1 JOHN 3:19

When we love others, we know we belong to the truth, and we feel at ease in the presence of God.

Announce to the nations, "The LORD is King! The world stands firm, never to be shaken, and he will judge its people with fairness." Tell the heavens and the earth to be glad and celebrate! Command the ocean to roar with

all its creatures and the fields to rejoice with all their crops. Then every tree in the forest will sing joyful songs to the LORD. He is coming to judge all people on earth with fairness and truth.   *Psalm 96:10–13*

57
Learn from History

The author of Ecclesiastes wrote, "Everything that happens has happened before; nothing is new, nothing under the sun. Someone might say, 'Here is something new!' But it happened before, long before we were born" (Ecclesiastes 1:9–10).

Things in life may seem new to us, but they aren't new to God. The same God who worked in the lives of people in biblical times is still working today. The things we struggle with—fear, doubt, insecurity, temptation, greed—are the things every generation has struggled with. Only the details change. When we look at how God worked in the lives of people in the past, we get a glimpse of how he can work in our lives.

Everything happens for a reason. Sometimes that reason is to teach new generations an old truth. ■

Take Time to Laugh and Cry
58

What time is it?

If your reference point is Ecclesiastes 3, that's a much more complicated question than it appears. According to the writer of Ecclesiastes, there is a season, a time, for everything—from birth and death to war and peace.

In verse 4, he tackled the seasons of our emotional landscape: "There is a time . . . for crying and laughing, weeping and dancing" (Ecclesiastes 3:2, 4).

His point is that both extremes are equally important to our emotional health. To laugh and dance is to celebrate the world around us, to express our joy at being alive. Laughter offers a much-needed release from the grim realities of our culture.

To cry and weep is to give vent to life's disappointments and pain, to mourn the passing of someone or something we love. These expressions of sadness initiate emotional healing. ■

And so, he will make you
happy and give you
something to smile about.

JOB 8:21

59 Know When to Be a Friend

In the seasons of life, there are times for hellos and times for good-byes, times for "embracing and parting" (Ecclesiastes 3:5).

The writer of Ecclesiastes was talking about something deeper than merely getting together with friends and then going home at a certain time. He's pointing out that sometimes friendships and relationships run their course.

There is a time for embracing a friend. We develop close relationships with people at different stages of life, as we share the joyful, painful, and even mundane moments of our lives together. New experiences in life often lead to new friendships.

There is also a time for parting. If you find that a change in your relationship status—say, a romance that's been downgraded to friendship—is too painful to bear or no longer productive, it may be time to part ways. If being with someone exposes you to temptations you'd prefer to avoid, it may be time to end the association altogether.

Painful though it may be, some relationships must come to an end. ∎

Speak When You Must

60

"Better to remain silent and be thought a fool than to speak out and remove all doubt." In recent history, this popular saying has been attributed to several famous leaders and authors, including Abraham Lincoln, Mark Twain, and Confucius.

The author of Ecclesiastes offered a similar thought thousands of years ago—and a little more gently: "There is a time for . . . listening and speaking" (Ecclesiastes 3:6–7).

We've all heard that principle before. We were just too busy talking to give it much thought. And why not? Talking has become our national pastime.

Turn on your television and you'll find talking heads, experts, and inveterate chatterboxes telling you what to buy, who to vote for, how to improve your health, and what to look for in a relationship. Social media and instant messaging encourage you to give voice to every thought the moment it occurs to you.

Amid this talk surplus, we face a critical shortage of listeners. And people's lives are emptier as a result.

When you listen to someone, you give that person a sense of value. You communicate the message that a person's thoughts, opinions, concerns, and experiences mean something to you.

Giving someone your undivided attention is one of the highest compliments you can pay. A good listener can bolster a person's dignity and self-respect. In some cases, a good listener can change someone's life. If you really want to make a difference in this world, learn to listen.

That's not to say all talk is useless. Ecclesiastes 3:6–7 emphasizes that there's a time for listening and for speaking. We need to understand, though, that speaking can take many different forms—some of which are much more valuable (and appreciated) than others.

Most valuable are the forms of speaking that focus on others: words of praise and encouragement; questions that inspire people to open up; solicited advice; and necessary confrontation and correction, such as a parent with a child.

Least valuable are the forms of speaking that spring from the desire to be heard, to make ourselves look good, or to make our opinions known. These include inane chatter, unsolicited advice, and cutting remarks. Avoid them at all costs. When it's time to speak, make sure your words are worth as much as possible.

Striking the right balance between listening and speaking will help you become a valuable resource to the people around you. ■

61

Find Satisfaction in Work

"I owe, I owe, so off to work I go." Good bumper sticker material. Lousy attitude toward work.

Words of
WISDOM

MATTHEW 5:16

Make your light shine, so others will see the good you do and will praise your Father in heaven.

Contrary to that popular sentiment, work is not a necessary evil or the means for funding the "good" things in life. Work is vital to our well-being. Without it, we cannot find genuine fulfillment.

The writer of Ecclesiastes put it this way: "I know the best thing we can do is to always enjoy life, because God's gift to us is the happiness we get from our food and drink and from the work we do" (Ecclesiastes 3:12–13).

God created us to enjoy work and derive happiness from it. One of the first things God did after creating humankind was to give us a purpose. "The LORD God put the man in the Garden of Eden to take care of it and to look after it" (Genesis 2:15). That assignment became part of who we are. God designed us to work.

After Adam and Eve disobeyed God and ate the forbidden fruit, his punishment struck at the heart of their identity. "You will sweat all your life to earn a living" (Genesis 3:19). From that point on, work became difficult for us. Yet God's punishment did not change the fact that we were created to find happiness and fulfillment in work.

God continues to promote work in his design of individuals. He created each of us to excel at certain kinds of tasks. Some of us thrive in settings where our creativity can run wild. Others do well in more structured environments. Some of us are excellent craftspeople; others are able to unlock the mysteries of science.

The point is, our talents and abilities—our God-given gifts—are tied intimately to the concept of work. God equipped us to find fulfillment in work in our own unique ways.

What is more, God also gives us the opportunity to bring glory to him through our work. "When you eat or drink or do anything else, always do it to honor God" (1 Corinthians 10:31). We should treat that opportunity like the high honor it is. When we are given the opportunity to work, we should put every one of our applicable God-given skills into it—because if God is honored, we will be blessed. ■

Find a Trustworthy

One of the absolute necessities of life is a trustworthy companion—a friend or spouse you can count on whether you're on top of the world or you've hit rock bottom. The writer of Ecclesiastes explained it this way:

> You are better having a friend than to be all alone, because then you will get more enjoyment out of what you earn. If you fall, your friend can help you up. But if you fall without having a friend nearby, you are really in trouble. If you sleep alone, you won't have anyone to keep you warm on a cold night. Someone might be able to beat up one of you, but not both of you. As the saying goes, "A rope made from three strands of cord is hard to break." (Ecclesiastes 4:9–12)

Though different people have different tastes in friends, some qualities are essential for a companion.

A companion faithfully supports you.

The friend described in Ecclesiastes 4 is one who will

- have your back when you're in trouble;
- bring stability, not chaos, to your life;
- encourage you and build your self-confidence;
- stick with you through the good and bad times.

Words of WISDOM

PROVERBS 27:17

Just as iron sharpens iron, friends sharpen the minds of each other.

Companion

62

This kind of friend won't
- toss you under the bus to save his or her own skin;
- undermine you behind your back with gossip and innuendo;
- second-guess you or make you doubt yourself;
- throw past failures in your face.

The only way you can know for sure whether someone will faithfully support you is to go through hard times together. The person standing next to you after most others have jumped ship is one you want for a companion.

A companion is strong.

The last thing you need is a companion who's a pushover. You need someone who will stay firm with beliefs and convictions. You need someone who won't fall with you when you stumble. You need someone who will challenge you when you need to be challenged.

Proverbs 27:17 says, "Just as iron sharpens iron, friends sharpen the minds of each other." You need a friend who doubles as an iron sharpener.

A companion brings out the best in you.

The ideal person to travel through life with is someone who
- knows your strengths and helps you play to them;
- helps you minimize your weaknesses;
- roots for your success;
- allows you to reciprocate. ■

63 Process Your Anger

The way we deal with anger reveals more about who we are than most of us would like to admit. That's the polite way of putting it. The writer of Ecclesiastes offers a more blunt assessment: "Only fools get angry quickly and hold a grudge" (Ecclesiastes 7:9).

To avoid a path that only the foolish tread, we must learn to process our anger in a healthy way. Here are a few tips to help you.

Practice your slow burn.

Grow a thick skin. When a potential provocation rears its head, consider the matter carefully. Decide whether it's really something worth pursuing. Learn to let inconsequential annoyances slide.

For reasons known only to them, some people are constantly itching for a fight—and any conflict will do. Don't allow yourself to be drawn into their orbit. Recognize their dysfunction for what it is, and refuse to engage them in conflict.

Say a quick prayer.

When the spark of anger ignites in you, turn to God. Ask him to keep your emotions from clouding your vision, to give you wisdom and guidance, and to bolster your self-control.

Talk to the person who's pushing your buttons.

Ask the pointed (and sometimes uncomfortable) questions that need to be addressed. Find out what the person's issues and motivation are. Ask yourself if the person has a legitimate beef with you. If so, make things right—to the best of your ability. Apologize and ask forgiveness.

Once you've dealt with your part of the conflict, you can talk about the other person's part. Explain—in a nonconfrontational way—why you're upset. Be open and honest. Try to get the person to see things from your perspective.

If the person apologizes, you can celebrate and thank God for a restored relationship. If not, you can—and should—leave the matter in God's hands.

Whatever the outcome, let your anger go as soon as your confrontation is over. Don't carry it into another day. Refuse to hold a grudge. The mental and emotional strain it causes is not worth whatever pleasure you may find in it. ■

Don't make friends with anyone who has a bad temper.
PROVERBS 22:24

WHY DO YOU FIGHT AND ARGUE WITH EACH OTHER? ISN'T IT BECAUSE YOU ARE FULL OF SELFISH DESIRES THAT FIGHT TO CONTROL YOUR BODY? YOU WANT SOMETHING YOU DON'T HAVE, AND YOU WILL DO ANYTHING TO GET IT. YOU WILL EVEN KILL! BUT YOU STILL CANNOT GET WHAT YOU WANT, AND YOU WON'T GET IT BY FIGHTING AND ARGUING. YOU SHOULD PRAY FOR IT.

JAMES 4:1–2

64 Choose the Right Path

You've likely heard real-life horror stories of people who followed the instructions of their GPS navigation devices straight into a lake or until they were hundreds of miles from their intended destination. The cost of following the wrong directions can be high. That's why the prophet Isaiah encouraged us to leave the navigation to God. "Whether you turn to the right or to the left, you will hear a voice saying, 'This is the road! Now follow it' " (Isaiah 30:21).

In Isaiah's time, the people primarily heard God's voice through his messengers, the prophets. Today we primarily hear God's voice through his Word, the Bible. The more we read it, the more we understand who God is and who he wants us to be. The more we pay attention to his Word, the clearer our path will become.

When we use God's navigation device—the Bible—we can often easily know we're listening to God, following his plan for our lives, and staying on the right path based on how our decisions line up with it. But sometimes knowing what to do along our life's journey isn't obvious and the signposts are less clear. We may be faced with two good choices that would equally seem to please God. How do we know which paths to take in those situations? Here are some traveling tips.

Take inventory of your backpack.

God equips each of us in a unique way. He's given us a one-of-a-kind set of skills, abilities, preferences, perspectives, interests, inspirations, motivations, and experiences. If we're traveling a route he's charted for us, those items will come into play. If, on the other hand, we don't feel as though we're making the most of our God-given talents, it may be time for some reflection.

Keep moving forward.

Very few paths follow a straight line from Point A to Point B. Some zigzag back and forth. Some rise gradually to impressive heights. Others drop so suddenly you may have difficulty keeping your footing. Regardless of the individual features, all paths ultimately run in one of two directions: either toward God or away from him.

Jonah, another Old Testament prophet, disobeyed God's instructions to him. He chose a path away from God and ended up in a fish's stomach for three days. It's always best to choose the path that leads toward God.

Beware of easy traveling.

Any experienced hiker, mountain climber, or skier will tell you that the best paths are often the most challenging ones. So it is with life. God makes a lot of promises in the Bible. One thing he never promises, though, is to make life easy for people.

Every challenge we face is an opportunity to grow and become stronger. Every pitfall that waylays us is an opportunity to learn and grow wiser. So, as odd as it seems, if your life's journey starts to become unchallenging and safe, it may be time to change paths. ■

65 Find Your Purpose

Jeremiah was an Old Testament prophet. His job as a prophet was to deliver messages from God to the leaders of Judah. Most of the messages Jeremiah delivered contained bad news: because the nation continued to turn its back on God, God was getting ready to deliver Judah to its enemies, the Babylonians.

No one likes to get bad news, especially the kind Jeremiah delivered—time after time after time. As a result, people began to blame the messenger. The leaders of Judah threw Jeremiah into prison, locked him in a cistern, and carried him away to Egypt. His family and friends rejected him. Still, the prophet kept coming back for more.

Why did Jeremiah endure such treatment? Why did he keep delivering messages that no one wanted to hear? Because that's what God created him to do. God said so himself. "Jeremiah, I am your Creator, and before you were born, I chose you to speak for me to the nations" (Jeremiah 1:4–5).

Jeremiah's unique physical, emotional, and spiritual makeup made him ideal for the job of prophet to Judah. God made sure of that. Jeremiah couldn't have found fulfillment or closeness to God doing anything else.

There's a lesson in Jeremiah's experience for all of us. God doesn't hand out assignments randomly. He creates us to carry out a certain work and makes sure we have everything we need to accomplish it. As a result, we cannot live a fulfilling life—or enjoy a close relationship with God—until we're doing what we're created to do.

What does that mean for you? What job did God equip you for—before you were even conceived? What strengths and abilities did he supply you with?

If you're still not sure of the answer, pray about it. Ask God to give you a sense of what he has in mind for you. If you already have that awareness, ask God for guidance in reaching where he wants you to be. If you're already there, take the plunge. Start using your gifts in ways that will please and honor him—and let his plan unfold around you. ∎

Learn to Keep and Give in Season

66

In the third chapter of his book, the author of Ecclesiastes introduced the notion that life has seasons—a time for everything, and everything in its time. His point is that genuine fulfillment comes from living "in season"—planting when it's time to plant and reaping when it's time to reap, crying when it's time to cry and laughing when it's time to laugh.

In verse 6, we find this season: "There is a time for . . . keeping and giving."

There are times when it is fitting to keep what you need for your current stage of life, whether it be material possessions, certain relationships, or other less tangible things. As a young adult, you may keep as many of your college friendships as you can, trying to hold on to the good times. You may keep your youthful restlessness and wanderlust. You may keep your interest in solo pursuits.

As an older adult, you may hold on to keepsakes of your children and grandchildren. You may keep memories of certain events so they aren't lost to history. You may keep friendships with people who connect you to your past.

At other times, you give away what you have in surplus. For some people, that may involve money, in the form of contributions, sponsorships, or scholarships. For other people, it may involve a surplus of time, talent, or provisions.

You give up what you no longer need. For some, that may include childhood collections—baseball cards, comic books, or jewelry. For others, it may mean giving up a partying lifestyle or friendships with people who no longer share your priorities.

At the heart of the purging process are the apostle Paul's words in 1 Corinthians 13:11: "When we were children, we thought and reasoned as children do. But when we grew up, we quit our childish ways."

As you rid yourself of things you no longer need, spend some time thinking about the roles they played in your life. What did each one cost you—not just in price, but in personal cost as well. What did you gain from it? How do you feel about it now? What did you learn about yourself from having it?

These are the questions that give us insight into ourselves and often result in some hard-earned wisdom. ■

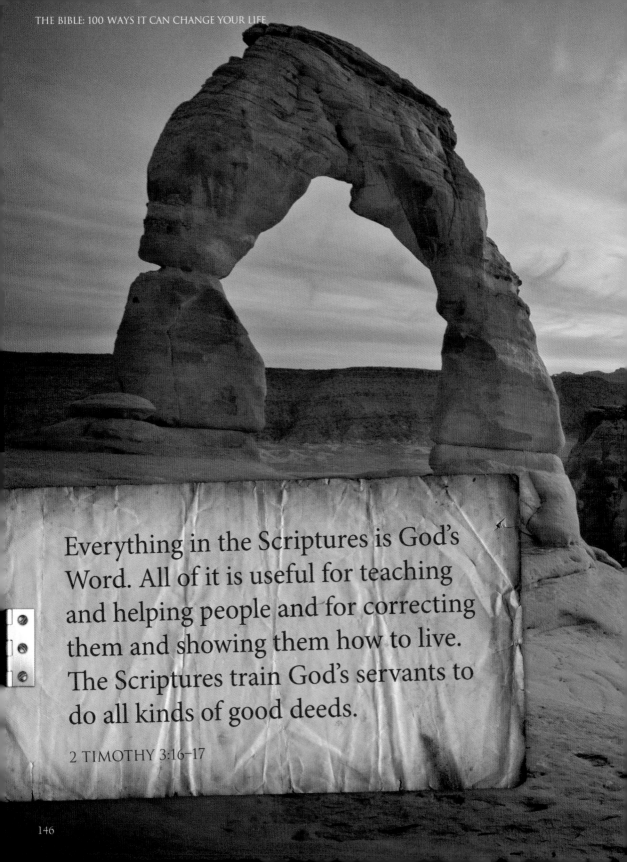

Everything in the Scriptures is God's Word. All of it is useful for teaching and helping people and for correcting them and showing them how to live. The Scriptures train God's servants to do all kinds of good deeds.

2 TIMOTHY 3:16–17

Be Bold

Shadrach, Meshach, and Abednego, three young Jewish men, were taken into captivity when Babylon conquered Jerusalem. Nebuchadnezzar, the king of Babylon, recognized the extraordinary potential in the three men and appointed them to important posts in his government. This special treatment angered the king's other advisers, who looked for a way to get rid of the Jewish interlopers.

King Nebuchadnezzar had created a giant gold statue and commanded everyone in his kingdom to bow down and worship it. Anyone who didn't bow down to the statue would be thrown into a fiery furnace.

On the appointed day, the statue was unveiled, and everyone in Babylon bowed to it, save for Shadrach, Meshach, and Abednego. This was the Babylonian advisers' chance to do away with the Jews. They knew that Shadrach, Meshach, and Abednego were forbidden by the God of Israel to bow down to any idols. So they alerted Nebuchadnezzar to the three Jews' disobedience.

Enraged, the king sent for them. He gave them one more chance to bow down to his idol and escape certain, painful death in the furnace. They politely declined his offer. No threat could make them disobey the God who had taken care of them throughout their captivity.

"The three men replied, 'Your Majesty, we don't need to defend ourselves. The God we worship can save us from you and your flaming furnace. But even if he doesn't, we still won't worship your gods and the gold statue you have set up' " (Daniel 3:16–18).

The essence of their faith is found in the words, "But even if he doesn't." They knew God could save them but didn't know if that's what he would do. It didn't matter, though. What mattered was obedience.

God did miraculously rescue Shadrach, Meshach, and Abednego from their fiery fate. Yet that's almost a coda to the real story. The point is that all three men stood ready to give their lives for what they believed in.

Perhaps you've never faced a life-or-death test of your faith. Perhaps you never will. You may, however, face tests that pull you out of your comfort zone. You may be asked to risk public embarrassment and vehement opposition for Jesus' sake. You may be put in uncomfortable positions.

How will you respond? Will you draw on the strength and courage that Shadrach, Meshach, and Abednego drew on to take your stand? ■

67

dare

dream

Fiery Furnace, 1266
Toros Roslin

68

FUTURE

Embrace

Embrace Your Calling

The Old Testament prophet Jonah could boast of something not many people have experienced: a direct, unmistakable, personal message from God.

"One day the LORD told Jonah, the son of Amittai, to go to the great city of Nineveh and say to the people, 'The LORD has seen your terrible sins. You are doomed!' " (Jonah 1:1–2).

And how did Jonah react to his irrefutable calling?

"Instead, Jonah ran from the LORD. He went to the seaport of Joppa and found a ship that was going to Spain. So he paid his fare, then got on the ship and sailed away to escape" (Jonah 1:3).

Big mistake. If you attended Sunday school as a kid, you probably know some of Jonah's story. He ran away because he hated the people of Nineveh and wanted God to destroy them; he didn't want God to give them a chance to repent. God sent a violent storm to rock Jonah's escape vessel. The ship's crew threw him overboard to deflect God's wrath. Jonah was then swallowed by a giant fish and vomited onto the shore three days later.

Belatedly and reluctantly, he headed to Nineveh to deliver God's message. And just as he feared, the Ninevites turned from their evil ways and escaped God's punishment. So the story of Jonah's calling ends happily for everyone but Jonah.

How will your story end?

Like Jonah, you have a calling—something you're uniquely equipped to do. Discovering that calling may take some time, but it's worth the effort.

A great starting place is to consider how you're uniquely gifted and where you've been placed. What are your God-given gifts and abilities? What experiences have shaped you? What preferences, quirks, and perspectives make you unique? How do people see you? How might your talents be put to use in your immediate environment? Where could they do the most good?

Once you have a sense of your calling—even if it's just a vague feeling that you should be putting certain skills to work—don't dismiss it. Embrace it. Pursue it.

You may not understand it. Your calling may run completely counter to your expectations—as Jonah's did. But give it a chance. You may find that it takes you places you never expected to go and gives you fulfillment and satisfaction you never imagined possible. ■

69 Recognize the Dignity in Everyone

It can be hard not to idolize the rich and powerful. But we need to pay close attention to the words Jesus spoke in his Sermon on the Mount: "God blesses those people who depend only on him. They belong to the kingdom of heaven!" (Matthew 5:3). Jesus emphasized the dignity and worth of people at society's margins. And in doing so, he gave us a model to follow.

In order to see people the way Jesus did, we need to keep three things in mind.

People are the creation of God.

Not everyone fits the same mold, but everyone was molded. We all bear the imprint of the Creator. We all have unique skills and God-given gifts. We all are much more alike than we might imagine.

Some people's unfortunate circumstances or poor life choices may cloud our view of them. If we look hard enough, though, we will still see God's handiwork in them. It's our responsibility to find it. Anyone who is created by God deserves our concern and our attention.

Everyone is on a journey.

Comedian Jimmy Durante once said, "Be nice to people on your way up because you meet them on your way down." Do you know people who have discovered the truth of that statement the hard way?

Every person's circumstances are fluid. What is true of someone today may not be true tomorrow. Fortunes change. Paths turn. People have the potential to be transformed.

Today you may be up and another person may be down. But that may not be the case forever. Who's to say that next year at this time your situations won't be reversed? So don't judge people based on their story up to this point. There's still too much to be written.

"Do unto others" is always your best bet.

When in doubt, always opt for the Golden Rule. Treat other people not as you think they deserve to be treated but as you would want to be treated in their position. Remember, dignity is one of the best gifts you can give anyone. ■

70

Undeserved Mercy

"The Gospel is good news of mercy to the undeserving. The symbol of the religion of Jesus is the cross, not the scales."

John Stott

Show Mercy

Any discussion of mercy must start with God's plan of salvation. Even though we deserve death for our sins, God gives us eternal life through the sacrifice of his Son. That's mercy—sparing people from the consequences they deserve.

According to Jesus, God loves mercy so much that he holds a special place in his heart for people who show it. "God blesses those people who are merciful. They will be treated with mercy!" (Matthew 5:7).

Jesus urges everyone who's experienced God's mercy to help others experience it. When we refuse to take revenge on those who hurt us—when we choose not to give people the punishment they deserve—we're giving them a very small taste of what God's mercy is like.

Keep his mercy fresh in your mind so that you'll be ready to show it to others. Once you've experienced genuine mercy, you must pass it on. ■

71

Give God the Credit

In sports, the chest-thumping athletes get most of the attention. The players who celebrate their own accomplishments are usually the ones who end up in the highlight reels.

In Jesus' Sermon on the Mount, though, it's the glory-averse people who get the spotlight. "God blesses those people who are humble. The earth will belong to them!" (Matthew 5:5).

God chooses to work through humble people because when he's done, they will make sure he gets the glory. They won't claim undue credit for themselves. That's why they are blessed.

Every positive thing about us is the product of God's creation. Every good thing we do is the result of God working through us. God uses us to make a difference in this world. ■

72

Comfort Those Who Grieve

God understands all too well why we mourn and ache after we lose someone close to us. That's why he promises to do something about it. Look at Jesus' words in Matthew 5:4:

"God blesses those people who grieve. They will find comfort!"

One of the ways God provides comfort to those in pain is by putting people in their lives. If you know someone who has suffered a loss, why not become an instrument of comfort and healing? Here are a few tips to help you.

Take the initiative.

The natural tendency is to put the ball in the grieving person's court by saying, "Let me know if there's anything I can do for you." However, there are two problems with that approach. First, the person may not feel comfortable approaching you for a favor. Second, the person may not know what he or she needs.

A better alternative is to do something without being asked: write a heartfelt card, prepare a meal, offer child-sitting or transportation services.

Avoid unhelpful words.

Many so-called comforting statements aren't worth the breath they require. Well-intentioned encouragements such as "You'll get through this" or "Things will be better tomorrow" are empty promises. There's no guarantee that either will happen, and no one knows that better than the hurting person. A preferable alternative is to say, "I will be here for you for as long as you need me."

You also want to avoid saying, "I know how you feel." You don't. No matter how similar your losses may seem to you, they are not the same. People respond to tragedy in many different ways. You cannot understand how people are feeling until they explain it to you.

Understand the value of your presence.

Sometimes words aren't necessary at all. Sometimes simply being there for another person—as a sounding board for the person's thoughts and feelings or as a silent partner in grieving—is enough. ∎

Words of WISDOM

2 CORINTHIANS 1:3–4

Praise God, the Father of our Lord Jesus Christ! The Father is a merciful God, who always gives us comfort. He comforts us when we are in trouble, so that we can share this same comfort with others in trouble.

Let your hope make you glad. Be patient in time of trouble and never stop praying. Take care of God's needy people and welcome strangers into your home.

Romans 12:12–13

73 Keep Your Heart Pure

Jesus' Sermon on the Mount laid the foundation for his revolutionary ministry. Intermingled with the groundbreaking teachings were some familiar themes, including his words in Matthew 5:8: "God blesses those people whose hearts are pure. They will see him!"

People whose hearts are pure—that is, people whose consciences are clean—share some common traits. For one thing, they listen to God. God's Spirit works through their consciences to let them know when something's wrong in their lives, whether it's a habit that's gotten out of control or an attitude that needs adjusting.

For another thing, pure-hearted people feel compelled to repair their relationship with God as soon as they feel a breach. They take advantage of God's readiness to forgive whenever they sincerely ask him for forgiveness. The idea of being separated from God for any length of time is unbearable to them.

Keep your heart pure by listening to God, allowing his Spirit to work through your conscience, and asking him to forgive you when you stumble. ■

Keep Your Eyes Pure 74

In our overly connected culture, pornography is as accessible as a weather forecast. Vast collections of erotic images are but a few mouse clicks away. To those who are tempted to click, Jesus offers a word of advice: don't.

Actually, what he said is this: "But I tell you if you look at another woman and want her, you are already unfaithful in your thoughts" (Matthew 5:28).

Pornography by its very nature disrupts intimacy between husbands and wives. Jesus' use of the word "unfaithful" was meant to underscore the sacred nature of the husband-wife relationship. To desire another person—even if that person is an image on a screen—is to stray from your spouse.

Pornography also distorts reality. From surgically enhanced and digitally altered bodies to wildly overacted and strategically edited sex scenes, porn offers a fictionalized version of what lovemaking is supposed to be. Its images follow you into the bedroom, creating unreal expectations that will leave you and your spouse unsatisfied. ■

STANDING FIRM

Ephesians 6:10-18

FINALLY, LET THE MIGHTY STRENGTH OF THE LORD MAKE YOU STRONG. PUT ON ALL THE ARMOR THAT GOD GIVES, SO YOU CAN DEFEND YOURSELF AGAINST THE DEVIL'S TRICKS. WE ARE NOT FIGHTING AGAINST HUMANS. WE ARE FIGHTING AGAINST FORCES AND AUTHORITIES AND AGAINST RULERS OF DARKNESS AND POWERS IN THE SPIRITUAL WORLD. SO PUT ON ALL THE ARMOR THAT GOD GIVES. THEN WHEN THAT EVIL DAY COMES, YOU WILL BE ABLE TO DEFEND YOURSELF. AND WHEN THE BATTLE IS OVER, YOU WILL STILL BE STANDING FIRM.

BE READY! LET THE TRUTH BE LIKE A BELT AROUND YOUR WAIST, AND LET GOD'S JUSTICE PROTECT YOU LIKE ARMOR. YOUR DESIRE TO TELL THE GOOD NEWS ABOUT PEACE SHOULD BE LIKE SHOES ON YOUR FEET. LET YOUR FAITH BE LIKE A SHIELD, AND YOU WILL BE ABLE TO STOP ALL THE FLAMING ARROWS OF THE EVIL ONE. LET GOD'S SAVING POWER BE LIKE A HELMET, AND FOR A SWORD USE GOD'S MESSAGE THAT COMES FROM THE SPIRIT.

NEVER STOP PRAYING, ESPECIALLY FOR OTHERS. ALWAYS PRAY BY THE POWER OF THE SPIRIT. STAY ALERT AND KEEP PRAYING FOR GOD'S PEOPLE.

Don't Retaliate

The Old Testament (Hebrew Bible) teaches the importance of a measured response. "An eye for an eye" meant that the punishment should fit the crime and not spiral beyond it into a vendetta. This rule also meant that, unlike the Code of Hammurabi belonging to Israel's Babylonian neighbors, the punishment didn't vary with one's social status: victim and perpetrator were to be treated as humans having equal value. The dignity of all humans was thereby elevated.

75

The ancient rabbis interpreted the biblical law as having meant an "eye price" for an eye; that is, their traditions indicated it meant a just fine should be imposed for the loss, not further mutilation.

Jesus went a step further:

> You know you have been taught, "An eye for an eye and a tooth for a tooth." But I tell you not to try to get even with a person who has done something to you. When someone slaps your right cheek, turn and let that person slap your other cheek. If someone sues you for your shirt, give up your coat as well. If a soldier forces you to carry his pack one mile, carry it two miles. When people ask you for something, give it to them. When they want to borrow money, lend it to them." (Matthew 5:38–42)

Jesus' way offers a high road—a way to stop the escalation of conflict. Yet, as with all his teachings, this one presents a challenge. To be specific, it's unnatural. In order to follow Jesus' instructions, we must actively resist our basic impulses.

Turning the other cheek requires more courage than any confrontation. To show kindness in a situation that normally inspires anger takes guts. In order to do it, you must shake your fear of being rejected or humiliated. You must risk the possibility of being taken advantage of or misunderstood. You must dare to look weak.

Yet the rewards are plentiful. There's a peace of mind that comes from knowing you've done everything you can to end a conflict. What's more, the person with the courage and character to turn the other cheek and go the extra mile for an enemy will leave a lasting impression on all who witness it. ■

Love Your Enemies

When you think of the word *enemy*, what images come to mind? Whose face do you see? Think of the circumstances that led to your present feelings about that person. Consider the relationship you have with the person today. And then compare your findings with Jesus' words in the first book of the New Testament.

76

You have heard people say, "Love your neighbors and hate your enemies." But I tell you to love your enemies and pray for anyone who mistreats you. Then you will be acting like your Father in heaven. He makes the sun rise on both good and bad people. And he sends rain for the ones who do right and for the ones who do wrong. If you love only those people who love you, will God reward you for this? Even tax collectors love their friends. If you greet only your friends, what's so great about this? Don't even unbelievers do that? But you must always act like your Father in heaven. (Matthew 5:43–48)

Jesus holds his followers to a different standard. You say you love the people who love you? So what? The worst people you know love their friends too.

If you say you love your enemies, though—and prove it with the way you treat them—you've set yourself apart. And that's exactly what Jesus wants his followers to do.

To love your enemies is to work toward the best possible relationship with them and to learn to live at peace with them. The first step in that process is to stop any ongoing escalation of anger. If the rift or circumstances that soured your relationship are fresh, address them in a positive way. Own up to your culpability in the matter, and give the other person a chance to do the same.

If the relationship can be salvaged, make every effort to do so. If not, draw on every bit of restraint and patience in you to establish a new attitude toward the person. If your supply seems low, ask God to refill it.

Refuse to respond in kind when the person insults or gossips about you. Instead, offer only kind words and good wishes. If you have an opportunity to help the person, take it. If you consistently follow Jesus' instructions, you likely won't have an enemy for long. ■

Invest Wisely

77

In our culture of Ponzi schemes and stock market fluctuations, how many careful investors can testify to the truth of Jesus' words in Matthew 6?

"Don't store up treasures on earth! Moths and rust can destroy them, and thieves can break in and steal them. Instead, store up your treasures in heaven, where moths and rust cannot destroy them, and thieves cannot break in and steal them. Your heart will always be where your treasure is" (Matthew 6:19–21).

Money is a resource from God; it's not a hedge against future disaster. Our responsibility is to put it to wise use—for others and ourselves. We must not depend on it, though, because it isn't guaranteed to anyone.

If we're serious about investing wisely, we must direct our time and attention to God's Word and his work. That's what will last. ∎

No one in Israel should ever be poor. The LORD your God is giving you this land, and he has promised to make you very successful, if you obey his laws and teachings that I'm giving you today. You will lend money to many nations, but you won't have to borrow. You will rule many nations, but they won't rule you.

Deuteronomy 15:4–6

Wisdom

PROVERBS 3:9–10

Honor the LORD by giving him your money and the first part of all your crops. Then you will have more grain and grapes than you will ever need.

78 Leave the Judging to God

If you were to ask a random sampling of people why they don't attend church, there's a pretty good chance you'd get an earful about hypocrisy. You'd hear about the audacity of pastors preaching about sin while carrying on extramarital affairs. You'd hear about the backbiting, finger-pointing, gossiping, and other ugly behavior that goes on behind the scenes in many congregations.

People can't stomach a holier-than-thou, judgmental attitude under the best of circumstances. But when that attitude comes from someone with issues that are just as bad as (or even worse than) their own, it's intolerable.

Jesus certainly recognized the danger of hypocrisy in the lives of his followers. Look at his words in Matthew 7:1–5:

> Don't condemn others, and God won't condemn you. God will be as hard on you as you are on others! He will treat you exactly as you treat them. You can see the speck in your friend's eye, but you don't notice the log in your own eye. How can you say, "My friend, let me take the speck out of your eye," when you don't see the log in your own eye? You're nothing but show-offs! First, take the log out of your own eye; then you can see how to take the speck out of your friend's eye.

Wisdom

ROMANS 2:1

Some of you accuse others of doing wrong. But there is no excuse for what you do. When you judge others, you condemn yourselves, because you are guilty of doing the very same things.

Any follower of Jesus who feels the urge to judge or point out flaws in someone else must do two things.

LOOK FOR—AND DEAL WITH— SIMILAR FLAWS OR WEAKNESSES IN OUR OWN LIVES.

If we want to confront someone for being a gossip, for example, we need to think first about the times we've gossiped about others. We need to think about the people we've hurt, the reputations we've damaged. We should seek out the people involved—the ones we were talking about and the ones we were talking to. We need to admit what we did and ask for forgiveness. While we're at it, we should ask God for forgiveness as well.

LEAVE ALL JUDGING TO GOD.

We don't have the moral authority to pass judgment on anyone. Nor do we have the omniscience to tell people what they should be doing.

Our best approach, then, is one of humility. We can offer to help others who are struggling with issues that are similar to those we struggle with.

Every person—including every churchgoer—struggles with weaknesses. Remember that worshiping God is the reason we go to church. Our focus should be on Jesus—the only perfect person who ever lived—instead of on the imperfect people who attend. ■

Treat others as you want them to treat you. This is what the Law and the Prophets are all about.

Matthew 7:12

Treat Others Well

Of all the rules in Scripture, only one has been dubbed "Golden." Jesus said, "Treat others as you want them to treat you. This is what the Law and the Prophets are all about" (Matthew 7:12).

The principle of this Golden Rule is simple enough to be taught in preschool Sunday school classes, yet difficult enough to challenge even the most mature believers.

The simplicity of Jesus' instruction is found in the application. If we're faced with a question of how to treat someone else, we need only ask what we would want in that situation—and act accordingly. The challenge is found in the ever-higher bar it sets. The more we demand of others in the way we're treated, the more that's demanded of us.

You'll notice there's no guarantee of reciprocity in Matthew 7:12. We don't treat other people well just so that they will treat us well. We treat others well because that's what Jesus' followers do. ■

Build on Something Solid

Jesus' words in Matthew 7 read like an announcement from the Emergency Alert System:

> Anyone who hears and obeys these teachings of mine is like a wise person who built a house on solid rock. Rain poured down, rivers flooded, and winds beat against that house. But it was built on solid rock, and so it did not fall.

> Anyone who hears my teachings and doesn't obey them is like a foolish person who built a house on sand. Rain poured down, rivers flooded, and the winds blew and beat against that house. Finally, it fell with a crash. (Matthew 7:24–27)

How strong is your spiritual foundation? What would happen if a powerful temptation suddenly bore down on you? Could you withstand a devastating financial crisis or the loss of a loved one?

Which of Jesus' teachings and truths could help shore up your walls and solidify your foundation? ■

81 Use Your Talents

Jesus was not one to spoon-feed his message to his followers. He wanted them to think about what he said, to wrestle with his meaning, and to figure out how to apply his words to their lives.

So he used parables—fictional stories that communicate real truths. One of his best-known parables (found in Matthew 25:14–30) concerns three servants who were put in charge of everything their master owned while he traveled for an extended period.

The master knew what each servant was capable of, so he divided his wealth accordingly. He gave the first servant 5,000 talents, the second 2,000 talents, and the third 1,000 talents.

While the master was gone, the first two servants doubled their amounts through wise investments. The third servant, however, hid his money in a hole in the ground. When the master returned, he was greatly pleased by the first two servants, who gave him back twice what he'd given them. But he was bitterly disappointed by the third, who gave him back only what he'd been given, nothing more and nothing less. He said to the servant, "You could have at least put my money in the bank, so I could have earned interest on it" (Matthew 25:2).

In order to understand the parable, we must recognize that we all have been given resources of time, talents, and material possessions by our Master—God. Some people have been given more than others. According to the parable, those people will have greater expectations placed on them. With great blessing comes great challenge. The relative amount of our talents doesn't matter, though; what matters is what we do with what we've been given.

First things first, though. The gifts we've been given are God's resources, not ours. They come from him and belong to him. And if we use them correctly, they will bring glory to him. If we don't acknowledge those truths, we run the risk of squandering our talents on ego fulfillment.

Our responsibility is to use our resources in valuable ways that will benefit others. Whether our talents involve writing, teaching, or caring for people, we can utilize them in ways that bring people closer to God, help them understand him better, or give them a tangible example of his love.

Jesus' parable teaches us that if we commit ourselves to returning a dividend on God's investment, he will bless and multiply our efforts. If we don't, we will have to answer for our negligence. ■

MATTHEW 25:14–30 The kingdom is also like what happened when a man went away and put his three servants in charge of all he owned. The man knew what each servant could do. So he handed 5,000 coins to the first servant, 2,000 to the second, and 1,000 to the third. Then he left the country.

As soon as the man had gone, the servant with the 5,000 coins used them to earn 5,000 more. The servant who had 2,000 coins did the same with his money and earned 2,000 more. But the servant with 1,000 coins dug a hole and hid his master's money in the ground.

Some time later the master of those servants returned. He called them in and asked what they had done with his money. The servant who had been given 5,000 coins brought them in with the 5,000 that he had earned. He said, "Sir, you gave me 5,000 coins, and I have earned 5,000 more."

"Wonderful!" his master replied. "You are a good and faithful servant. I left you in charge of only a little, but now I will put you in charge of much more. Come and share in my happiness!"

Next, the servant who had been given 2,000 coins came in and said, "Sir, you gave me 2,000 coins, and I have earned 2,000 more."

"Wonderful!" his master replied. "You are a good and faithful servant. I left you in charge of only a little, but now I will put you in charge of much more. Come and share in my happiness!"

The servant who had been given 1,000 coins then came in and said, "Sir, I know that you are hard to get along with. You harvest what you don't plant and gather crops where you haven't scattered seed. I was frightened and went out and hid your money in the ground. Here is every single coin!"

The master of the servant told him, "You are lazy and good-for-nothing! . . . You could have at least put my money in the bank, so that I could have earned interest on it."

Then the master said, ". . . Everyone who has something will be given more, and they will have more than enough. But everything will be taken from those who don't have anything. You are a worthless servant, and you will be thrown out into the dark where people will cry and grit their teeth in pain."

Look at the Heart 82

Throughout his ministry, Jesus had to deal with opponents who wanted to embarrass and discredit him. The irony is that his most vociferous enemies were the religious leaders of Israel—the very people who should have embraced him.

In first-century Jewish culture, religious leaders were the pillars of the community. They were considered to be wiser, more learned, and more spiritual than everyone else. Jesus, however, saw them in a different light. He called out to them, "You are a bunch of evil snakes, so how can you say anything good? Your words show what is in your hearts" (Matthew 12:34).

Jesus' point remains relevant for his followers today. People's reputations in the community mean little compared to the words and deeds that flow from them. If you want to know what's in people's hearts, listen to what they say—and watch what they do. ■

Love Unselfishly

"Love isn't selfish" (1 Corinthians 13:5).

The apostle Paul's words in this verse will likely hit a nerve with people who have found themselves in a one-sided relationship. Some may question whether a truly unselfish relationship is even possible.

To commit to an unselfish relationship is to put the other person's needs ahead of yours. Some recipients will be humbled by such a sacrifice and will work hard not to exploit it. Others, though, will treat it as a license to indulge—an invitation to a power trip.

That kind of imbalance is unhealthy and is not what Paul intended. If the unselfishness continues to be one-sided in a relationship, repair or reevaluation must be done. One person devoted to unselfish love eventually will become disillusioned. Two people devoted to unselfish love will create a bond for the ages. ■

83

My dear friends, we must love each other. Love comes from God, and when we love each other, it shows we have been given new life. ~ 1 John 4:7

84
Choose Kindness

In 1 Corinthians 13, the apostle Paul put love under the microscope to determine what it is and isn't, what it does and doesn't do. His first conclusion?

"Love is . . . kind" (1 Corinthians 13:4).

If that seems like a bland sentiment at first glance, look again. Kindness is not the same as niceness. To be kind to people is to interact with them in a way that makes them comfortable. To be kind is to divest ourselves of sarcasm, brusqueness, and a judgmental attitude.

The kindness Paul was talking about rejects the notion that familiarity breeds contempt. To be kind is to give people a sense of their worth. To be kind is to make them feel—in a very sincere way—that they have a special place in your heart.

To be kind is to leave people feeling good about the time you spent together. ∎

GOD LOVES YOU AND HAS CHOSEN YOU AS HIS OWN SPECIAL PEOPLE. SO BE GENTLE, KIND, HUMBLE, MEEK, AND PATIENT. PUT UP WITH EACH OTHER, AND FORGIVE ANYONE WHO DOES YOU WRONG, JUST AS CHRIST HAS FORGIVEN YOU. COLOSSIANS 3:12–13

85 Learn to Trust

In 1 Corinthians 13, the apostle Paul presented an ideal—but not idealized—model of love. Every quality he listed is achievable through work, including this daunting challenge: "Love is always . . . trusting" (1 Corinthians 13:7).

If you've been burned by a relationship in the past, you understand how difficult it can be to trust others. Yet love compels us to try. The best strategy is to start slowly, to entrust people with things that can't be used against you. If they prove themselves trustworthy with those smaller things, then you can work up to riskier kinds of trust.

As you work to trust others, though, you must also work to be the kind of person others can trust. Give value to your word. When you commit to something, no matter how small or insignificant it may seem, honor that commitment. Refuse to traffic in excuses and apologies. ■

86 Honor Your Parents

The relationship between parent and child holds tremendous importance in the eyes of God. In the Old Testament, God gave his people the Ten Commandments to obey. Number five on the list, and the first dealing with human relations, is "Respect your father and your mother, and you will live a long time in the land I am giving you" (Exodus 20:12).

We also find this commandment in the New Testament. The apostle Paul repeated it for emphasis: "The first commandment with a promise says, 'Obey your father and your mother, and you will have a long and happy life' " (Ephesians 6:1–3).

To respect and obey healthy, loving parents is to listen to them—to seek their input on important matters. That's not to suggest that as an adult you must do everything they say, but you should consider their advice.

It is also possible to respect and obey dysfunctional parents without being drawn into their dysfunctional orbit. You can do this by

- understanding their dysfunction;
- recognizing their limitations;
- giving them the opportunity for reconciliation;
- forgiving them. ■

EPHESIANS
6:1-3

Be Open to Correction

87

In his letter to the Galatians, the apostle Paul described an astonishing confrontation between two titans of early Christianity. Paul recalled the time he was forced to confront the apostle Peter—one of Jesus' closest friends— about Peter's views.

When Peter came to Antioch, I told him face to face that he was wrong. He used to eat with Gentile followers of the Lord, until James sent some Jewish followers. Peter was afraid of the Jews and soon stopped eating with Gentiles. He and the others hid their true feelings so well that even Barnabas was fooled. But when I saw they were not really obeying the truth that is in the good news, I corrected Peter in front of everyone and said:

Peter, you are a Jew, but you live like a Gentile. So how can you force Gentiles to live like Jews? . . .

When we Jews started looking for a way to please God, we discovered that we are sinners too. Does this mean that Christ is the one who makes us sinners? No, it doesn't! But if I tear down something and then build it again, I prove that I was wrong at first. It was the Law itself that killed me and freed me from its power, so I could live for God.

(Galatians 2:11–14, 17–19)

St. Peter Preaching in the Presence of St. Mark, c.1433
Fra Angelico (c. 1395–1455)

The issue was complex, but what it boiled down to was this: Peter, a Jew, wanted Gentile Christians to start following Old Testament Jewish laws, which was something that Jesus never required.

Peter's actions and attitude were causing confusion and hard feelings among Jesus' followers, so Paul did something about it.

It took courage for Paul to correct Peter. Peter was wrong, and he needed to know that his attitude was causing damage in other people's lives. Peter learned from Paul's correction and grew in his faith as a result.

We can learn an important lesson from it too. If the apostle Peter wasn't above correction, we certainly aren't either. If someone has the courage to sincerely and lovingly confront us about something we do or believe, we would be wise to listen. The moment we start to think we're above being disciplined or corrected, we're in serious trouble. ∎

88

Don't let anyone make fun of you, just because you are young.

Don't Be Fooled by Age

Timothy, a friend of the apostle Paul, served as the pastor of a first-century church in Ephesus. The problem was that Timothy was younger than many people in his congregation. That's why Paul felt compelled to encourage him with the following words: "Don't let anyone make fun of you, just because you are young. Set an example for other followers by what you say and do, as well as by your love, faith, and purity" (1 Timothy 4:12).

That verse carries two important implications for us.

We must not judge people based on their age. Young children can teach us important lessons if we allow them to. So can senior citizens, who have a wealth of experience to draw on.

We must not allow people to dismiss us based on age. Each of us has a unique set of insights and experiences to offer, regardless of our birth year. ■

Isaiah 48:17

I am the holy Lord God,
the one who rescues you.
For your own good,
I teach you,
and I lead you
along the right path.

89

PROVERBS
3:5–6

WITH ALL YOUR HEART YOU MUST TRUST THE LORD AND NOT YOUR OWN JUDGMENT. ALWAYS LET HIM LEAD YOU, AND HE WILL CLEAR THE ROAD FOR YOU TO FOLLOW.

Trust God

Learning to trust God is not easy to develop. Too many things work against having a lasting faith, including inexplicable tragedies, personal setbacks, and everyday, run-of-the-mill doubt.

Through it all, though, we need to remember the apostle Paul's words in Titus 3:4–7: "God our Savior showed us how good and kind he is. He saved us because of his mercy, and not because of any good things we have done. God washed us by the power of the Holy Spirit. He gave us new birth and a fresh beginning. God sent Jesus Christ our Savior to give us his Spirit. Jesus treated us much better than we deserve. He made us acceptable to God and gave us the hope of eternal life."

Where our lives are concerned, God has earned the benefit of the doubt. If we let go of the wheel and turn control over to him, he will steer us to where we belong. ■

> "NEVER BE AFRAID TO TRUST AN UNKNOWN FUTURE TO A KNOWN GOD."
>
> CORRIE TEN BOOM

90 Protect and Serve

In 1 Corinthians 13, the apostle Paul compiled a list of the qualities of ideal love, including this nugget: "Love is always supportive, loyal" (1 Corinthians 13:7).

Paul was writing about protection. To love someone is to involve yourself actively in keeping that person from harm—both from within and without. Physical danger is an obvious starting point, but the protection Paul wrote about runs much deeper than that.

If you love people, you will not keep secrets from them. You will not allow others to destroy their confidence or self-image. You will not stand idly by while other people take advantage of them.

If addiction is a problem for someone you love, you will be proactive in addressing it. You will talk to experts and find the best course of action.

If you truly love people, you will protect them from everyone who seeks to do them harm—including themselves. ■

91 Put Action behind Your Words

Jesus told the story of a Jewish man who was robbed and savagely beaten while traveling (Luke 10:29–37).

As he lay by the side of the road, a Jewish priest passed by, noticed the man, and kept walking. A Jewish temple worker also noticed the man and kept walking. The beaten man appeared to be dead. It is possible that the two temple officials avoided the apparent corpse so they wouldn't become ritually impure and thereby ineligible to perform their temple work for an entire week (Numbers 19:11). But because they didn't check to make sure, they missed the chance to help the man.

The third person to pass by was a Samaritan. Historically, the Samaritans and Jews had a hostile relationship, yet the Samaritan did not behave as one might have expected. Instead, the Samaritan treated the man's wounds, put him on his donkey, transported him to a local inn, nursed him back to health, and then gave the innkeeper money to continue taking care of the man after the Samaritan left.

The priest and temple worker might have felt compassion for the man, but the Samaritan did something. That, according to the apostle James, is evidence of genuine faith. "My friends, what good is it to say you have faith, when you don't do anything to show you really do have faith? Can this kind of faith save you? If you know someone who doesn't have any clothes or food, you shouldn't just say, 'I hope all goes well for you. I hope you will be warm and have plenty to eat.' What good is it to say this, unless you do something to help?" (James 2:14–16).

The priest and temple worker claimed to have faith but did not act to help. Genuine faith involves more than just words; it involves action. If you'd like to put action behind your words, here are a few quick tips for becoming a difference maker in people's lives.

KEEP YOUR EYES AND EARS OPEN.

There are people hurting in your community, workplace, school, and church. The best way to discover their needs is to talk to them and listen to them. The more available you are to the people around you, the more aware you'll be of their needs.

KEEP SELF-PROMOTION TO A MINIMUM.

Don't call attention to yourself when you offer assistance to others. The fact that you help people doesn't make you a hero; it makes you a faithful follower of Jesus. The fact that he knows what you're doing should be attention enough.

DO IT AGAIN—AND AGAIN.

Be as consistent as you can in putting actions behind your words. Do your best to make helping others a habit in your life. ■

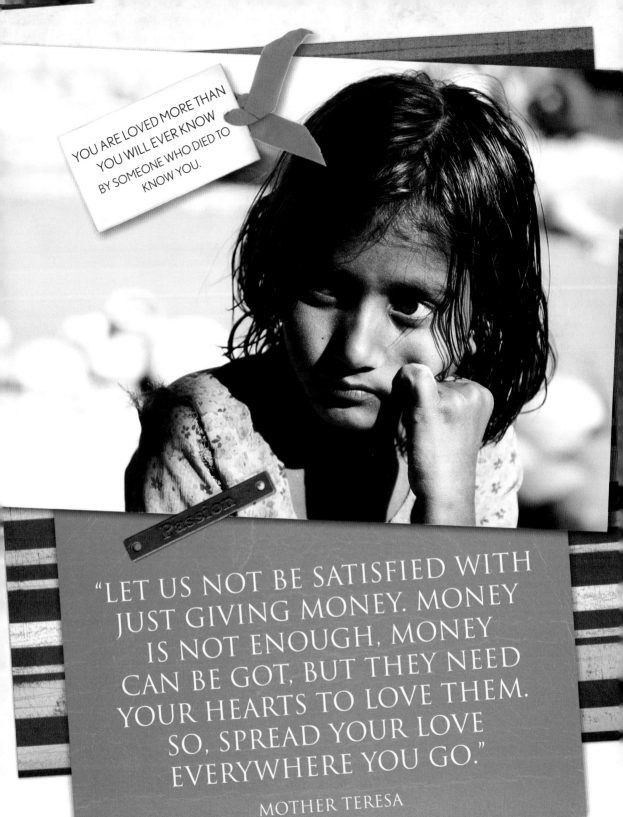

YOU ARE LOVED MORE THAN YOU WILL EVER KNOW BY SOMEONE WHO DIED TO KNOW YOU.

Passion

"LET US NOT BE SATISFIED WITH JUST GIVING MONEY. MONEY IS NOT ENOUGH, MONEY CAN BE GOT, BUT THEY NEED YOUR HEARTS TO LOVE THEM. SO, SPREAD YOUR LOVE EVERYWHERE YOU GO."

MOTHER TERESA

friendship (frend·ship) the state of being friends 2. a mutual union or bond felt between people who care deeply for one another

92

Be Ever Ready

Not everyone recognizes God's truth when they see or hear it. Their personal beliefs or past experiences may make it difficult for some people to accept the idea of a loving Creator, much less a Savior.

The apostle Peter encouraged followers of Jesus to prepare for inevitable interactions with such people: "Always be ready to give an answer when someone asks you about your hope" (1 Peter 3:15).

You'll notice that he wasn't instructing us to defend the finer points of Christian theology (although it will make our task much easier if we at least know the basics). He simply wanted Christians to be able to explain, in convincing terms, the answers to the following questions:

- Why does the Bible's message make sense to us?
- Why have we chosen to follow Jesus?
- What has happened in our lives as a result of our relationship with Jesus?

Can you do it? ■

"You tried to harm me, but God made it turn out for the best . . ."
Genesis 50:20

93 Focus on What Is Good

Joseph's family was a model of dysfunction. His father, Jacob, loved Joseph more than his other eleven sons—and made no effort to hide his favoritism. That inspired hatred in Joseph's brothers. One day, in a moment of anger, they sold Joseph into slavery in Egypt.

With God's help, though, Joseph didn't stay a slave. Eventually he became second-in-command in Egypt and helped prepare the nation for a terrible famine. When the famine struck, Joseph's brothers came to Egypt looking for food. Imagine their horror when they realized Joseph was the man in charge.

Joseph put their minds at ease with these words: "You tried to harm me, but God made it turn out for the best, so that he could save all these people, as he is now doing" (Genesis 50:20).

Those words still apply. God can—and will—work good from evil. Count on it. ■

Go Ahead and Ask 94

The name *Job* has become synonymous with suffering—and for good reason. God allowed Satan to take away Job's children, his wealth and possessions, and his health. Job was left a broken and miserable man.

Understandably, Job had some questions for God. He had faithfully served the Lord his entire life, and he wanted to know why God would allow such terrible things to happen to him. Job was in misery and wanted answers.

God began his response to Job with two simple, yet very pointed, questions: "How did I lay the foundation for the earth? Were you there?" (Job 38:4).

God's message was clear: You're not capable of fully understanding who I am and what I do.

God isn't offended by our questions and doubts. In fact, he encourages us to bring them to him. Yet our inability to understand him should never prevent us from trusting him. ■

95

Risk Faithfulness

While the Jewish people were in exile in Persia, Daniel served as an adviser to the Persian king Darius. Darius's other advisers hated Daniel and devised a way to get rid of him. They convinced Darius to outlaw prayer to anyone but the king and to sentence violators to death in a pit filled with starving lions.

> You have been faithful to your God, and I pray that he will rescue you.
> Daniel 6:16

In response to the law, Daniel went home, knelt in front of a window facing Jerusalem, and prayed, giving thanks to God. Immediately he was arrested and taken to the lions' den.

The king realized he'd been duped, but he couldn't change his law. As Daniel was thrown into the pit, Darius told him, "You have been faithful to your God, and I pray that he will rescue you" (Daniel 6:16).

And that's exactly what happened. God rewarded Daniel's faithfulness and saved him from the lions.

How will God reward your risky faithfulness? ■

96

Ask, Seek, Knock

Prayer is so mysterious. It gives us direct access to God and allows us to communicate with him in a personal way. Our praise and thanks reach him; his guidance and direction reach us.

One aspect of prayer in particular—supplication, the requests we bring to God—defies easy explanation. Jesus gives us a starting point in Matthew 7:7: "Ask, and you will receive. Search, and you will find. Knock, and the door will be opened for you."

Yet this is no blank check. God won't give us something that will ultimately harm us, no matter how many times we ask. What he will give us is an understanding of his will. According to the Christian faith, God has given his Spirit to those who follow Jesus to help us reach that understanding.

God's Spirit assists us in praying by helping us put words to our thoughts and desires. The Spirit also works to align our thinking with God's thinking, so that the things God wants become the things we want. ■

ask, seek, knock

Wisdom

E. M. BOUNDS

"God shapes the world by prayer. The more prayer there is in the world, the better the world will be, the mightier the forces against evil ..."

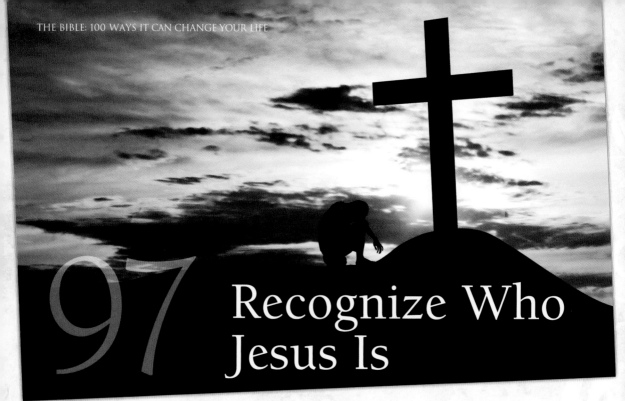

97 Recognize Who Jesus Is

During the three hours that Jesus hung on the cross, darkness covered the land even though it was midday. A great earthquake split rocks and opened tombs. Dead people came back to life. Amid such unprecedented occurrences, one realization was inescapable: "The officer and the soldiers guarding Jesus felt the earthquake and saw everything else that happened. They were frightened and said, 'This man really was God's Son!' " (Matthew 27:54).

Since most of us do not experience miraculous occurrences such as the soldiers witnessed, how do we reach the same conclusion? And what is more, how do we help others recognize that Jesus is the living Son of God, that he was more than just a good teacher, a wise philosopher, a controversial reformer, or an unknowable character shrouded in the mists of ancient history?

That's the challenge Jesus' followers face every day. Are you willing to meet that challenge today? What will you do to better know who he is? ∎

> Christ is exactly like God, who cannot be seen. He is the first-born Son, superior to all creation.
>
> Colossians 1:15

98
Have Faith

Are you a person of faith? Have you ever stopped to consider what that means? The writer of Hebrews gives us a working definition of faith that we can build on: "Faith makes us sure of what we hope for and gives us proof of what we cannot see" (Hebrews 11:1).

Beyond that, we can add certain other truths.

FAITH IS A RISK.

To believe in Jesus is to put all our eggs in one basket—to follow his way at the expense of all others, including our own.

FAITH IS A WORK IN PROGRESS.

What seems certain today may seem less so tomorrow. Where faith goes, doubts follow. The keys to strengthening our faith are prayer and Bible study.

FAITH IS REWARDED.

In John 20:29, Jesus says, "The people who have faith in me without seeing me are the ones who are really blessed!" ■

99 Fight the Winning Battle

Why do bad things happen to good people—specifically, to God's people? Though the apostle Peter didn't answer the question directly, he did shed light on the issue to help us see things from a different perspective. "Count it a blessing when you suffer for being a Christian. This shows that God's glorious Spirit is with you" (1 Peter 4:14).

We assume that following Jesus will bring happiness, joy, healing, and fulfillment. And sometimes it will. Sometimes, though, it will bring opposition and people who hate us simply because of our faith. To follow Jesus is to set ourselves apart, which is something that always carries risks and consequences.

The good news is, our future is set. Jesus won the war against sin and evil. Yet until we are in heaven, individual battles will rage on. The fact that we are battling—and suffering blows—means we're on the right side. ■

1 CORINTHIANS 9:24–27

YOU KNOW THAT MANY RUNNERS ENTER A RACE, AND ONLY ONE OF THEM WINS THE PRIZE. SO RUN TO WIN! ATHLETES WORK HARD TO WIN A CROWN THAT CANNOT LAST, BUT WE DO IT FOR A CROWN THAT WILL LAST FOREVER. I DON'T RUN WITHOUT A GOAL. AND I DON'T BOX BY BEATING MY FISTS IN THE AIR. I KEEP MY BODY UNDER CONTROL AND MAKE IT MY SLAVE, SO I WON'T LOSE OUT AFTER TELLING THE GOOD NEWS TO OTHERS.

100
Believe the Truth

> EVERYTHING IN THE SCRIPTURES IS GOD'S WORD. ALL OF IT IS USEFUL FOR TEACHING AND HELPING PEOPLE AND FOR CORRECT-ING THEM AND SHOWING THEM HOW TO LIVE.
> 2 TIMOTHY 3:16

BELIEVE (be·leve´) 1. to put one's trust in 2. to accept on as fact 3. to have faith in

The Bible must be true. That statement carries a dual meaning—both of which are vital to everyone who follows Christ.

The Bible must be *true* . . . because it is drawn from eyewitness accounts. The apostle Peter, one of those eyewitnesses, testified to one aspect of its veracity: "When we told you about the power and the return of our Lord Jesus Christ, we were not telling clever stories someone had made up. But with our own eyes we saw his true greatness" (2 Peter 1:16).

Every other Bible writer would offer similar testimony. They either heard directly from God or witnessed the person of Jesus.

The Bible *must* be true . . . because our faith is built on it and our lives are changed because of it. Everything we know about God, his Son, sin, salvation, discipleship, and eternal life comes from its pages because they were inspired by God's own Spirit. God's Word is the lifeblood of Christianity.

Our faith is secure because the Bible is true. ■

FLOWERS AND GRASS FADE AWAY,

BUT WHAT OUR GOD HAS SAID

WILL NEVER CHANGE.

ISAIAH 40:8